FINDING
MARTHA'S PLACE

My Journey Through Sin, Salvation, and
Lots of Soul Food

MARTHA HAWKINS
with MARCUS BROTHERTON

A TOUCHSTONE BOOK
Published by Simon & Schuster

New York   London   Toronto   Sydney

Touchstone
A Division of Simon & Schuster, Inc.
1230 Avenue of the Americas
New York, NY 10020

This work is a memoir. Certain names and characteristics have been changed,
and some characters are composites.

Scripture quotations taken from: King James Version, The New International Version
Colorado Springs: International Bible Society (1978–1984)

First Touchstone hardcover edition January 2010

TOUCHSTONE and colophon are registered trademarks of Simon & Schuster, Inc.

For information about special discounts for bulk purchases, please contact Simon &
Schuster Special Sales at 1-866-506-1949 or business@simonandschuster.com.

The Simon & Schuster Speakers Bureau can bring authors to your live event. For more
information or to book an event contact the Simon & Schuster Speakers Bureau at
1-866-248-3049 or visit our website at www.simonspeakers.com.

Designed by Ruth Lee-Mui

1   3   5   7   9   10   8   6   4   2

Library of Congress Cataloging-in-Publication Data
Hawkins, Martha.
Finding Martha's Place My journey through sin, salvation, and lots of soul food /
by Martha Hawkins ; with Marcus Brotherton.
p.   cm.
1. Hawkins, Martha. 2. Hawkins, Martha—Philosophy.
3. Martha's Place. 4. African Americans—Alabama—Montgomery—Biography.
5. African American women—Alabama—Montgomery—Biography.
6. Restaurateurs—Alabama—Montgomery—Biography. 7. Divorced mothers—
Alabama—Montgomery—Biography. 8. Montgomery (Ala.)—Biography.
9. Montgomery (Ala.)—Race relations. I. Brotherton, Marcus. II. Title.
F334.M753 H394 2010   976.1'47063092 B—dc22   2009022945

ISBN 978-1-4391-3788-8
ISBN 978-1-4391-5590-5 (ebook)

To my mama and daddy,
Willie and Sallie Hawkins.

You never stopped believing in me.
Where would I be today without
your hope, prayers, and unending love?

Contents

Welcome to
Martha's Place

SOME FOLKS HAVE TOLD ME they feel an actual tingle when they walk through the front door. Others simply say that when you step inside, someone's apt to call you by name as like as not. Still others say there's some kinda magic around here—but I don't know nothing about that.

What I do know is that every day come late morning, maybe fifteen minutes before we open, I gather whoever's on shift in the kitchen with me, maybe Beryl and Rosalee, and we all hold hands family-style like we're sitting around a lunch table at home, and we look upward. That's what this restaurant is built on, 'cause that's all we know to do. We pray out loud, all at the same time, no shushing or uppityness when we talk to the good Lord. If another person's praying then the rest of us are pursing our lips and saying mmm-mmm Amen and Thank you, Jesus and Yes, Lord let it be so. Every morning, that's how it goes.

I hope all this talk right up front about praying doesn't bother you. I know plenty of folks who ain't praying folks, and if that's your story I ain't here to convince you otherwise. I figure it takes plenty of courage to not be the praying kind, so the Lord bless you if that's the way you are. Still, I hope you don't mind getting prayed for beforehand if ever you come into my restaurant. Every morning we're praying that these walls will bring peace to all inside. We're praying that our customers will know comfort and rest. And we're praying for folks anywhere who might be feeling poorly or desperate or may be just in need of a smile. I don't think you'll mind all that praying, if you think about it. In all my years yet, I ain't heard nobody complain about getting prayed for, even if they're not the praying kind.

So where do you find this restaurant? Well, if y'all ever visit Montgomery, Alabama, be sure to head downtown to the old part of the city and hop aboard the Lunch Trolley Express. The ride is free and you'll enjoy some good sights. The trolley takes you down Church Street past Troy University and the federal courthouse building; you'll make a left jog onto Sayre Street, and you'll stop right outside a restaurant where the sign in front reads MARTHA'S PLACE RESTAURANT & CATERING SERVICE. When the weather's warm we keep an old wheelbarrow next to that sign with flowers blooming in it. Pinks and yellows and lavenders, and I'm right proud of that sign, though it's not getting any younger and I see it needs new paint again this year.

Truly, this old restaurant ain't much to look at on the outside. But it's got character, it rightly does. It's in the first house on a street of two-story, wood-sided houses. We've got wood shutters on the windows and a big old wraparound porch out front. Across the street is a parking lot with a chain-link fence, and two down is a day care, and right next door you'll see the Inner City Church of Christ, a tan brick building with six huge white-painted Greek columns out front. Those are our neighbors. Inside the restaurant is the main dining room that looks just like a living room with a fireplace and mantel and hardwood floors all weathered and worn. The artwork all shows rural Southern life, paintings of sharecroppers bringing in the cotton, of folks walking to church way out in the country, of folks having picnics in the fields.

It's a funny thing about this little old restaurant: it seems to have created quite a stir. I don't rightly understand it all myself. A newspaper recently described it like this: "For dignitaries, movers and shakers, and people who simply want a great lunch, Martha's Place in Montgomery has become known as a mandatory place to eat."

Well, that sounds highfalutin to me, but it's true that we've had our share of dignified folks walk through the door. In the entryway there's a picture of world heavyweight champ Evander Holyfield in a white shirt and tie placing an order here. Whoopi Goldberg, Sissy Spacek, Walter Matthau, Nell Carter, Macaulay Culkin, Angela Bassett T.D. Jakes, Kirk Franklin—they've all eaten the food from Martha's Place. There's a picture of Ted Koppel and me arm in arm in the dining room. Lots of politicians have stopped by, even the governor of Alabama, and plenty of professional football players, business folk, artists, and musicians.

History is part of this place, too. Rosa Parks used to be a regular before she passed. Missus Parks was real soft-spoken, you never could imagine her being the cause of so much change. She always took corn bread muffins to go. CNN held the ceremonies for the fortieth anniversary of the Montgomery bus boycott at Martha's Place.

Plenty of regular folks come here too. Everybody's welcome. They call what we serve up comfort food. If you walk through the front door at lunchtime you'll smell turkey and dressing if it's Wednesday, fried pork steak if it's Thursday, barbecued pork if it's Friday, and steak and gravy come Tuesdays. Mondays we're closed because I usually cater Saturdays and often Sundays and then I need one day per week that's just a day for Martha. Any day of the week, you're also welcome to enjoy a big helping of Southern fried chicken, which ain't no ordinary fried chicken neither. It's hot and juicy on the inside with tender, crisp outsides, and it ain't never greasy. When you eat a piece of my fried chicken you can snap your fingers afterward. Then there's chicken and dumplings and collards and fried green tomatoes and pork chop casserole and baked ham and steamed rice and smothered cabbage and black-eyed peas. For dessert there's pound cake and apple cobbler and banana pudding and sweet potato pie and strawberry pie and more.

Over the years I can't believe all the fuss that this little restaurant has created. Food critics tend to praise it all up and down. Reporters sometimes praise what they call the ambience; sometimes they talk about the unlikely story behind the restaurant. Martha's Place has been written up in the *New York Times, Oprah Magazine, Southern Living, Essence, Guideposts,* and a bunch of those *Let's Go* books for folks coming to visit America from other countries. I've been on National Public Radio. Some college textbook has a write-up about this restaurant in it, something about economic know-how or American business success stories, I guess. Another writer has words of mine alongside those of Camille Cosby, Phylicia Rashad, and Della Reese in a big old New York book called *Dear Success Seeker: Wisdom from Outstanding Women.* Shoot, there's even a museum out in California that's got a Martha Hawkins exhibit in it. Someone told me about that, though I've never seen it myself.

Me, well, I'm still thinking about what I got to do for this day. At 4:30 I'm up, preparing the menu for this day's opening. In a few hours folks will be coming in to eat. On busy days the line will stretch out the door. Corn bread and homemade cobbler welcome everybody so they'll feel that they're pretty near right at home. That's my kind of success. That's all I've wanted, for that's always been my dream.

Then there's public speaking too. I never imagined or dreamed about that, but this restaurant has opened some doors for me so that I seem to be talking quite often these days—women's groups, sorority chapters, clubs, church groups, that type of thing. There's business groups too, some big corporations—even the CEO of Sam's Club came to Montgomery after hearing me speak. Seems he wanted to taste the food in this restaurant for himself. I doubt it was my words that persuaded him. It's the good Lord who sprinkles extra sauce upon my words. That's what I'll say.

And of course my boys—they're my real success. In the entryway there's a picture of my oldest, Shawn, shaking hands with the president of the U.S.A. My other boys, too—Quint, Reginald, Nyrone—they all done me real proud, so proud. But I'll tell you more about that to come.

Things weren't always this way with Martha Hawkins. I guess that's what makes my story something to tell. I had to overcome a heap of trouble to find this success today. Some folks would call my restaurant the picture of the American dream, but I know it involves more. Ask me today what the secret to success is and I'll tell you that it's not about where you are from, or how you got to where you are, but about whether you can step into God's promise for your life. That's the secret I've found. It's made all the difference between failure and success, poverty and prosperity, sadness and happiness, even life and death.

Let me see if I can describe success in ordinary terms, something I'm real familiar with. When I think of success I like to think of lima beans, one of the regulars on my menu. Most folks will tell you that they never met a lima bean they liked, and I can value that, for most lima beans are not worth the heap of dirt they was growed in. But lima beans are on my menu for a reason.

When you think of lima beans they're usually small and shriveled, all tumbling lost at the cold end of a bag of mixed vegetables. Folks will say that no lima bean never amounted to much. But the lima beans at Martha's Place are just plain different. Why, a fella from up Mississippi ordered a bowl just the other day. He was a big fella with a ruddy face and white suit, no stranger to eating I guessed, and suspicious at first at the bowlful of beans I brought him, wrinkling his nose and wiping his brow like it was gonna take a lot of work to choke them down. He forked up one, tasted it, then he got this particular smile on his face. "Martha," he said, "these lima beans are downright luscious," and he wolfed that bowl down and asked for another. That's the word he used: luscious. I've heard my lima beans described as a lot of good things before, but I ain't never heard no one describe my lima beans as luscious.

So this is what you'll taste if you ever order yourself a bowl. The lima beans at Martha's Place are cooked with a whole lot of love. When you put them against your lips they feel plump, like you was smooching the back of your baby grandson's knee. The beans are soft and piping warm, straight out of the pot they was cooked in. They're cooked in together with a lot of good country butter, and flavored with salt and pepper and a few kitchen secrets only a handful of folks know. And if you close your eyes and let them, those lima beans will remind you of sitting at home with all the people you love, and on the supper table in front of you is spread a country banquet on a red-checked cloth, and all of your friends are enjoying themselves and diving in and helping themselves and joking together and having a good old time.

Those lima beans are on my menu because I know how food can become more than just food. It's what a body uses for change. Like crackers and grape juice passed around at church, food can become what centers things when everything has gone astray. You take something as poor and lonely as a lima bean—on one hand it's ugly and stupid and forlorn and forgotten. But then you cook it just so, and a powerful change happens. Lima beans become something luscious—the food of delight and flavor and faith.

That's why they're on my menu at Martha's Place. That's the poetry of this restaurant's life, my life, my success, this food that smacks of hope. And that's what I aim to show you in the pages to come. It'll take some time to get there. We've got to pass through some mighty dark waters before we come to the light. But we'll get there soon. Hope is right around the corner, I promise. It's right there on the table with a warm cake pan of corn bread. There's a mound of soft butter and side plate with your name on it. And next to that is a glass for receiving. And a frosty pitcher full of ice-cold lemonade.

FINDING MARTHA'S PLACE

I

Shocked

Jackson Hospital,
Montgomery, Alabama
1975

I JUST WANTED TO FORGET.

Forget. Forget. Forget.

Mama went with me to the hospital. Somebody else drove. Mama didn't drive. She never did. I couldn't tell you who drove. Daddy never drove neither. So it might have been one of my older sisters or brothers. Everything was blurry in my mind. All I saw was the black back of someone's head in the front seat while Mama sat close to me in the back. Maybe it was winter. Or maybe it was spring. It didn't matter much to me. I wasn't doing much of anything these days. I wasn't even cooking. The building loomed up big and white in front of us as the car drove into the circular driveway. Then we was under a large awning with skylights,

I think, because shafts of glowing came down around us like spot-lights. The car's door handle felt cold as I closed the door behind me. It was strangely chilled for Alabama's usual heat. Mama took my arm and we started walking although I felt like sitting. A smile crossed my face as the doors opened for us. I wanted to be here.

After I had had my nervous breakdown, the doctor had sug-gested I stay at Jackson Hospital for a while. We had tried every-thing else. Talking. Therapy. Pills. I took a heap of pills. The names jumbled together in my mind, colors and letters, z's and ph's and Thorazines and benzodiazepinesomethingorothers. You know that feeling like when you've had a few drinks, maybe a second or third past where you normally stop, and you want to shake the straw out of your head but you can't? That's how I felt, 'cept I felt like that all the time. Like that, and like I wanted to lie down even though it might have been the middle of the day. And whenever I did my eyes closed and I saw shapes and swirls and folks' faces and I heard voices and laughing. And other folks might be in a room with me and talking to me but I was just sitting on a couch looking at a cor-ner in the ceiling because that's the only place it felt safe to look, and maybe I was just imagining those other folks there in the room with me after all.

She needs to go to the hospital for a rest, was what I remembered hear-ing the doctor say. A rest sounded good to me, so when Mama and I took the elevator to the fourth floor at Jackson, I was surprised to see a sign that read PSYCHIATRIC WARD. Was that where I was going? Oh well. Mama musta known. She signed the papers at the admitting desk for me. A white lady sat behind the high counter. Her voice sounded far away. "No visitors," she said. "And no phone calls . . . at least for a while." I wanted to hug the lady. To have her smile at me. I think she did when the doors at the end of the hall buzzed open for us. "The doors are locked for safety reasons," the lady had explained to Mama. That was a surprise to me. It felt scary to think that they were keeping all those crazy folks locked in there.

Mama and I passed through the buzzing doors and found my

room. I saw it was just a regular hospital room and my shoulders relaxed a bit. There was no padded walls like I had feared, just a room
with high, white-painted walls and a bed, a chair, and side tables.
Mama unpacked my suitcase and pulled the blinds down. It must
have been the afternoon sun she needed to keep out for me. I felt
her lips press on my forehead as she kissed me good-bye. "I'll talk
with you later, Honeychild," she said. Her voice sounded so good.
Just warm and familiar. It reminded me of dessert. Mama was always
cooking. I wanted to forget a lot of things, but I never wanted to
forget that. What was my favorite dessert? I had to think about that
one. It was a toss-up between bread pudding and red velvet cake.
Probably the bread pudding. Yeah, that was it. That's one thing
Mama made all the time. She took leftover bread or biscuits and put
raisins and pineapples on top. She could always reuse bread if it was
left over. She cooked it and added a raisin sauce. It was sugary and
creamy. No, I didn't want to forget bread pudding. Some things you
don't ever want to forget.

When Mama left the hospital room I was all alone. I looked at
the walls, at my suitcase that stood empty now near the door, my
clothes were stored away somewhere in the room. What was that
sound I heard? It must have been a cat. Someone had let a kitty cat
run loose in the hospital. What kind of a crazy place was this? Who
would have let a cat into a hospital? It wasn't one of those shrieky
toms that lurk around your window when you're trying to sleep and
let loose with those awful wails. It was more like a kitten. A tiny
kitten's mew. That's what I heard. There it came again. Maybe it
was a baby's cry. A tiny, kittenlike baby's cry. Maybe my room was
nearby the maternity ward in this hospital. Did they let crazy folks
near babies? Oooh I liked seeing babies. I hoped I'd see one soon. I
put a hand over my mouth. My lips were open and now I knew the
mew was coming from me. My face was wet and hot and I looked
for a Kleenex but there was none. I sat down on the bed. My mew
kept coming and I couldn't stop it then. The cry became more high
pitched, more nasal. My body was shaking now. Maybe I was just

cold. I pulled my feet up on the bed, my knees bent, and wrapped the blanket around me. The cry was still coming from my mouth. I knew it wouldn't stop for a while. My crying seldom did. I burrowed my head into the pillow. It was firm and flat and clean, not fluffy like my pillow at home. All around me I felt the emptiness of the white walls and the darkness of the drawn blinds. Soon the pillow was clammy and damp from my crying. For hours, that's all I could see and feel.

When I woke a nurse was taking my pulse. It might have been morning. Maybe it was night. She wore a white V-neck top with a starched collar. Her head was covered and her butterscotch hair bunched out from underneath her swan hat. I loved blond hair. I always have. The nurse's eyes were blue and she was young, mid-twenties, about the same age as me. She wrote something on a chart and stroked the top of my head. "You just lie and rest," she said. Her smile was genuine. "The doctor will be in soon."

Something about the color of the pretty nurse's hair sparked another memory, my favorite toy as a child. I'd want to hold on to that memory too. I was five and had crafted a doll out of some old twine I found, a newspaper, and an empty Coca-Cola bottle. The twine became the doll's hair. For hours I had sat combing and pleating that hair. Beige, golden, blond hair—just like a real princess. She didn't have no name, my doll, she was just pretty. Pretty Doll, maybe that's what I called her. I made Pretty Doll out of twine because we never had money for real toys except at Christmas, and Christmas was a long way off. It must have been spring when I made the doll because I was sitting outside on our high, high steps and the Alabama sky was blue above me. We lived in an old house then. It was a hot day with one or two pearly clouds floating by, but not too hot a day yet even for Montgomery. Joe, our brown-and-black collie, his chest and legs a furry silver, was lying on his front paws with his tongue sticking out panting, his head cocked in my direction, a smile on his doggy face. I liked Joe a lot. He was keeping a protective eye on me, I'm sure. There was a fence around our yard, and we kids weren't allowed to play outside of that fence except for roller skating. Every kid in our neighborhood had those old metal strap-ons that sparked fire when you skated hard. It made you feel so alive to roller-skate, you'd be skating so hard and your side would ache and you'd be breathing in gulps—and we ventured outside the fence on the concrete sidewalks for that. But usually we were inside the yard where it was safer, using a piece of broken glass to scratch hopscotch squares in the dirt. On summer evenings all my family sat around on the inside of that fence. We laughed and told stories and sang. Neighbors were with us. It was so hot on those nights and we sweated in the summertime air. Nobody had air conditioners so we made fans out of cardboard to keep the heat at bay. At night we burned rags on our lawn to keep mosquitoes from biting. The smoke served that purpose. I don't know how my parents coaxed the rags to burn for so long like they did, if they dipped them in oil or water to smoke, or what it was. We children surely couldn't mess with fire, we wasn't allowed. And maybe somebody had whipped up home-made ice cream with the berries in season. Mmmmmm. I licked my lips. Blueberry ice cream. We made homemade blueberry ice cream nearly every Sunday and ate it all together by our little campfire of rags. Yes, I'd hold on to those memories if I could. I'd grip to them tightly. Some things you don't ever want to ever forget.

After that, doctors and nurses filed in and out of my room regularly. Maybe a couple days passed. Maybe more. I saw Pretty Nurse whenever her shift came around. She remembered my name. *Martha.* I liked how she said it, sweetly, a whisper almost. I had been told what they was admitting me for. I had been taking a lot of medication for my nerves but wasn't getting no better. The doctors said that they had this alternative treatment, sometimes it really did a number for people to help them feel better. That sounded good to me.

It must have been a week after being admitted that the treatments began. They happened right in my room. The doctors and nurses came in with this machine. They rolled it in with its metal wires and electrodes. A nurse slathered ointment on the sides of my head. It wasn't shaved. My chin-length kinky hair was still there and my temples felt oily, like she had plastered on a slick type of lard. Then they put something steel around my head and clamped it into place. I reached up and felt a metal coil sticking out from my hair. Nurses took my arms and strapped them down and also my legs so they wouldn't jerk. I stayed awake, lying in my hospital bed, not sitting in an electric chair as I had thought might happen.

Electroconvulsive therapy was the preferred name, I figured, because somebody said it with a low voice. A nurse gave me some more pills and I swallowed them with a sticky throat. They turned the machine on, I almost laughed to think that the lights might dim. It would have been a crazy cuckoo laugh, I'm sure, where the swollen river inside me would spill its banks at last, bust loose with nervous hilarity, and run and run and run forever. But I didn't laugh then. I didn't say a word.

I guess the treatments had begun because a nurse said, "You're having one now." There wasn't no blast of volts, no sudden lightning or raised, stiffening body. Just a little zap, then another, and another, a few seconds each at a time. The shocks felt like I had shuffled across a carpet with my socks on then touched something metal, but the shocks came stronger than that, like I was having little seizures. I tried to count how long each one lasted. One second, two, three, four, five, six seconds. And then it was over. Then came another. One second, two, three, four, five, six. And it was over. Then another. Then the pulses of current stopped. "That's all for today," I heard a doctor say. His voice sounded high above me near the ceiling. "We'll do it again tomorrow." Pretty Nurse was there with me also, stroking my head, holding my hand, removing the electrodes from my temples. I was crying then. "Just sleep," Pretty Nurse said. "Close your eyes, Martha, and sleep." She sounded like my mama. Maybe she was.

I was never quite sure what was real for a while after that. I saw images in my head. Pictures as if in a photo album. We had this old basketball hoop in the backyard. My backyard, I mean, not my parents' house where I grew up but the little house I rented for my kids now. I worked at the glass company most days when I wasn't sick, and so after I paid for day care and food we could afford a bit nicer house in an okay neighborhood although bills always made my chest tight. I saw that basketball hoop again and again. Maybe I was there in my backyard. Maybe I was still lying in my hospital bed. Most days when my sons came home from school I watched them play basketball in that backyard. I hoped I was there.

Shawn, at twelve, was my oldest son. He was the protective one, the man in charge. Once near Christmas a few years back Shawn had found me crying. "Why, Mama?" I could hear the plea in his voice. "What are you crying so much? How can we help?" I had told him I was worried about money for Christmas presents. That was partly the truth, as much as I figured a young boy could bear to understand. "We got plenty of toys, Mama," Shawn said. "Honest. We don't need no more Christmas presents. Really, we don't." Shawn was always on the short side, which he hated, and he had asked me to order him something from the catalog that he could put in his shoes to help him be taller. I don't remember if I was able to buy Christmas gifts that year or not.

Quintin, my next son, was quieter, maybe more fearful. At ten he was always afraid something would happen to me. He told me that outright. A boy shouldn't have to fear that for his mother. His favorite song was the same as mine. Whenever Otis Redding came on the radio, we cranked up the tune and danced throughout the house: *That changes gotta come, now / Oh yes it is, my oh my oh my oh my.*

Reginald was tall and slender even by age eight. He was the mischievous one, always into stuff he shouldn't be into, always sticking out his tongue, always saying a cuss word or whatever young boys wasn't supposed to say. Goodness, how I wanted to see him, to hold him. I wanted to see them all so badly.

Nyrone was my baby. At age six he was happy and jolly, a little bundle of jokes and songs. He was always roly-poly even from birth when he weighed in at just under nine pounds. They didn't allow my boys to see me in the hospital, so maybe it was all just a dream. The basketball hoop in the backyard. If it was a dream I didn't want to wake from this one. Sometimes if I felt well enough I played basketball with my boys, just to let them know their mama wasn't through yet. Or if they played and their friends came over, I fixed them some corn bread or something. No matter how poorly I felt I could always fix something. I loved it when I could get out there in the evening air with them and pass and shoot and give high-fives when the ball swished through the rim. I loved it that my boys played basketball in our backyard. Basketball knitted us together as a family. Seeing them there with the backyard hoop was a way of knowing where they was and that they were safe. I'm sure all mothers feel that. Even if they're a bit crazy. I always wanted to take care of my sons.

Doctors had explained to me, as best as I could understand, that the main reason for the shock treatments was to get to the root of the problem and help my depression. The theory was that if I could forget, I wouldn't be depressed anymore. And there lay all the conflict I felt inside. If you forget some stuff, the bad stuff, the painful stuff, well that's good, right? But there's the strong chance that you can forget more stuff than you want to. You forget the good stuff too. And I didn't want to lose that. I needed all the good stuff in my life.

They told me it was a controversial treatment. Supposedly you could improve a mood disorder by altering the electrical activity inside your brain. Electroshock therapy was designed to do that, hopefully without damaging any mental function in the process. It worked for some folks. It really did. But sometimes the side effects took over, they said, and that was one of its risks. Yes. And there were more. They warned me the shocks could produce headaches, dizziness, and seizures. The memory loss, both short-term and long-term, would come more as a side effect. No one was quite sure how long a memory loss would last. Or if by not remembering I'd actually feel happy again. But that was the hope, anyway. Strangely, losing my memory was the one side effect I wanted most. Yet it was also the one side effect I fought against the hardest.

They gave me five shock treatments spread over five days. I don't know if they upped the volts each day. The pills they kept giving me swirled around my brain. I fought against the fog, searching for something bright. Little flashes of sunbeams came to me, calling me from out of the mist, memories I wanted to cling to, images and faces I desperately wanted to sort out and keep. From the blur in my mind I heard the voice of Martin Luther King, of all folks. I had heard him speak at the Oak Street Baptist Church when I was maybe fourteen. My daddy took me and my brothers and sisters to hear him. Everybody knew who he was. We couldn't get in because there were so many folks at the church so we had to stand outside and listen from a loudspeaker hung on a pole. Hearing that man of so much thunder and power and gentleness and hope was exciting and scary at the same time. Reverend King reminded us that we needed to stick together, that it was a time for change, and to never forget what we hoped for. I'd file that memory away if I could.

One morning in the hospital I put my lips on a drinking glass and remembered my first kiss. The memory just came to me, pure and unblinking. I was fourteen. There were no stars or anything in the kiss, but I'd file that memory also as one of the good ones. The kiss came from Reuben, a boy in my neighborhood where we lived in the projects. He was seventeen and friends with my brother Edward. My brother and I had gone to a basketball game at school. Reuben met us there because Daddy would have never allowed me to date at that age. Afterward Edward walked me home. I would have gotten into trouble if Reuben had walked me home. So Reuben just walked with us and my brother was a good friend and walked ahead of us so he couldn't hear or see while Reuben and I lagged back thirty yards and Reuben held my hand. I liked him okay. He was known around school as a real cool dude. Sure, I liked the association that brought. He always dressed nice with his pressed slacks and his white shirt tucked in, and he always wore a fedora angled down on his face, all jaunty and James Dean. He was going to graduate that year and then go into the Air Force. Whew. When

Reuben let go of my hand there on the road he turned and faced me. I felt those flip-flops in my stomach like it was right before a quiz in math class. Then he smushed his face against mine and it was all over. He walked one way and I caught up to my brother and walked the rest of the way home with him.

Mama was cooking when we got home. She was always cooking. Give her a pot of peas and a dash of salt and she could make a meal for the entire neighborhood. Coming through the front door I smelled fresh-baked corn bread, squash casserole, and smothered cabbage. Maybe there'd be sweet potato pie for dessert. I hoped. The taste of Reuben's lips was still in my mouth and I had a wedge in my throat that I didn't feel right about. When you grow up thinking some things are wrong and then you cross that line, or maybe you haven't even crossed a line but you're pretty sure that your mama and daddy would disapprove of your actions if they found out, that can be hard to swallow. I didn't say anything. Not just then. If Reuben wanted to date me, he would need to come by and ask Daddy's permission. I certainly wasn't going to do it for the boy.

Other memories that floated through my mind in the hospital weren't as clear. They battled through my head day after day. Some I fought to keep. Many I fought to rid myself of. I won't talk about those just yet. After the fifth and final shock treatment all I felt like doing still was lying down in bed. Pretty Nurse came by one morning around then, felt my forehead, and asked me if I wanted the blinds opened. "Martha," she said, very quietly, very gently, "it's a beautiful day outside. Just come and look. I'll help you over to the window so you can see." I so wanted to look with Pretty Nurse. I wanted to want to anyway. I wished I could sit up in bed, shake my curls loose and hold on to the hand she held out to me. But I shook my head. At least I responded to her. That was something wasn't it? I so liked the outside. My favorite time of the year in Montgomery is when the trees change color. Maybe it was autumn right now. Sometimes I walked the forty-five minutes to Oak Park near the central part of downtown. We was allowed in there nowadays.

There was a fishpond there by the side of the park where it was quiet, and I took bread with me when I remembered to and threw it to the fish so they could bubble up and get it. They weren't catfish; if they were catfish somebody would be out there trying to catch them. They were brightly colored fish, maybe koi. I sat on the side of the concrete pond and could often think there best. But today I didn't even want to look outside.

Not the next day neither.

They tell me that four weeks went by while I lay in bed at Jackson Hospital. I drifted in and out for hours at a time. I felt like a zombie. It must have been near the end of my stay when I finally was allowed to phone Mama from my room and it changed everything. I had just washed down a handful of pills and Mama sounded so happy to hear me.

"Mama," I said. My voice was woozy. "Uncle Roosevelt is here at the hospital. He came to visit me. He's knocking on the door outside. He wants to come in. He keeps knocking, Mama. What should I do?" My head felt burning, blistering, the room was boiling, surging.

"You don't let him in!" Mama hissed. "Martha, do you hear me! Whatever you do, don't let him in."

"But Mama, I said, "Uncle Roosevelt really wants to come in. He's knocking so loud. He keeps knocking and knocking."

"Martha! You listen to me!" Mama's voice rose to a shout. "Your Uncle Roosevelt had a stroke several years back. You know that! He's dead, Martha! Uncle Roosevelt's dead! Whoever's knocking on your door, you don't let him in! You hear!?"

It must have been the medication talking. There was nothing wrong with Uncle Roosevelt. He never done me no wrong. He wasn't a nightmare. Only a hallucination.

The next day after Uncle Roosevelt wanted to stop by, Mama came and got me. She signed me out of the hospital and we went home to her house. She propped me up on the couch in the living room and went into the kitchen. I could hear pots and pans clanging and dishes being rattled back and forth. Mama must have been starting to make supper. The living room was dark, an oppressive, gray-dark color. Or maybe that was just me. My head hurt. My stomach hurt. My body hurt. One thing was certain: those shock treatments hadn't done a thing. Any bad thing I wanted to forget was still in my head. I could just make out the words to an old spiritual Mama was singing in the kitchen. Maybe she was humming it and the words were still in my mind. *There's a balm in Gilead to make the wounded whole / Gonna kick my wings and cleave the air / I'm gonna lay down my heavy load.*

Maybe that was hope enough for today. For the first time in weeks I closed my eyes and really slept.

2

How We Was

LET'S JUST LET ME SLEEP there for a while, shall we? Lord knows I could use it. Let's just let me lie on the couch asleep in my memory while I tell you some things about my life. It's important you know how I got to there. And it's much more important that you know how I got from there to here. *Today*, that is. Because today is a fine day and much more fine than the days of yesterday. And I'll say right now that even though I was shocked and drugged and depressed and lying on my mama's couch with four boys to look after and no husband to love me and harder things than that ahead, which I would shortly go through, this book has a happy ending after all. That's why I'm writing this down today. There would be hope for me, from where I came from and what I went through and what my life is like now—and there's hope for you too. No matter how dark the waters may seem, I know there's hope.

For you to really understand what I was so desperately trying to forget, I need to take you back even farther in time, and you need to know that many years ago in the rural outlie of Alabama my grandmother became sick. This was no ordinary sickness, for my grandmother sensed within her it was a sickness unto death. I don't know where my grandpa was, for I never knew him nor met any of my grandparents. So my grandmother called over to her a young man in the community and told him that he needed to marry her daughter Sallie. Willie Hawkins was twenty-one years old, and Grandma's daughter Sallie was just fourteen when the marriage was proposed, but Willie Hawkins evidently knew a good thing when he saw it for he married Sallie straightaway. Yes, there was an older daughter in the family but she was sickly as well, so it was Sallie who was strong and was married. There were four younger boys in Grandma's family and Sallie and Willie set out to raise those boys until they could all look after themselves, for sure enough my grandmother soon passed and they was left all alone.

Willie and Sallie Hawkins were to become my parents, yet there were many seasons to be gone through before I came along. My grandmother had chosen Willie Hawkins to marry her daughter because the boy had a job and jobs were scarce in 1926, the year they was married. My daddy picked cotton and he worked around the plantation as a farmhand when the cotton wasn't ripe. He drove tractors and worked with sugarcane and pulled the peanuts off the vines. Mama and Daddy lived in an old house that sat way off the ground, and my sisters will tell you that Mama gave them cookies and they were allowed to go up under the house to play. Daddy made 25¢ a day but he was a smart man and a hard worker and when he became married he asked the man for a raise, and soon Willie Hawkins made 35¢ a day for five days of work per week, even though he worked much more than that for the man.

The increase in cash money came as a real blessing, small as it was, because Willie and Sallie Hawkins soon had children of their own in addition to the four boys they were already raising. Back then everybody had big families. It was babies, babies, babies, nothing but having babies and along came Georgia and Rosalee and Willie Jr. and Alberta and Wylie and that meant five children for a family total of eleven with the four boys they was already raising. Daddy talked to the man again and mentioned that he had nothing to fear on the farm with Daddy taking care of things, and soon Daddy was making 50¢ per day. That meant a whole $2.50 per week, $10 a month. It was 1935 then, and if any employee at any job normally made the $100 per month that was sort of regular for a man to expect, then he could save up the $600 it took to buy a car or the $3,000 it cost to buy a house of any repute. But Daddy picked cotton so he wasn't buying no cars or no houses, and it was the thick of the Great Depression so nobody was thinking about buying much of anything, job or no job.

Daddy rode a bicycle when he needed to get somewhere. He never did learn to drive. A loaf of bread cost 8¢ and a pound of hamburger could be bought for 11¢, but Mama wasn't buying none of those things neither. She planted a garden and raised chickens and collected their eggs, and there was always good country butter because there was a cow, and Daddy was able to get himself some hogs too. So with the fare from Mama's garden and the bacon and chicken, the Hawkins family always managed to eat okay. You have to realize how good it is to eat fresh collard greens straight from the garden. If you're from the North and have never seen a collard green, you got to know it's like spinach, which doesn't sound very tasty at first unless you're Popeye. But you mix in whatever you have with the collards, and whatever you usually have on hand in the South is country butter and bacon. It's not ordinary bacon neither, not like them scraggly pieces you get nowadays in restaurants no sir, this bacon is thick as a shingle and loaded with all the drippings of good grease, and you stir in a piece of that real hog bacon with the collard greens and then you get some of that country butter and mix that in too and you got plenty of that because the cow gave plenty of milk that morning. Mmmm mmm. That's some fine eating.

Now, if you've never heard folks talk about country butter then you don't know what you're missing neither, for this is a real staple of Southern cooking and where I am from folks are always raving about country butter: Whoo whee it's country butter this and country butter that. Once I heard about a Northerner who had come to the South for a spell who was trying to learn himself about the culture. He had the audacity to ask what was so special about country butter. Or maybe his question was simply what was so different about country butter with all the raving we did about it. Well if you has to ask then you don't need to know; that's how the folks responded to his question. But I will let you in on a little secret and if you promise not to tell; the difference that makes it so good is how country butter is churned and how country butter is fresh and how it comes from a cow that has been enjoying itself in a field all day eating things that the good Lord caused to grow wild. That's country butter, and if you ever go to the Deep South today you be sure to ask for some, you hear?

Back to the cash money that Daddy was making. Or rather that he wasn't. Mama was pregnant again and there was surely more children to come after that, so in time Daddy figured there was no way his family was going to be a success on his wages from picking cotton. He heard there were new jobs at a fertilizer factory on the north end of Montgomery so he hired a truck and packed the family and they moved from the country to the city. That's why they left: because Daddy felt he was worth more.

In their new home they stayed just down the street from the factory and Daddy could ride his bike there for his new job. From their house you could put your hand to your eyes and look away far between the trees and see the Alabama River flowing blue and brown, and down the street was St. James Baptist Church #2 with its red bricks and stained glass, and in the neighborhood were lots of foundries and cement buildings and the Whitfield Foods manufacturing plant, which made syrup among other things, and a coal yard for heat for when you could afford it, and a café run by a woman named Missus Watts, and a great pickle factory with its huge shiny round steel tanks out front. If you ever had a few cents you could walk to the pickle factory and buy a pickle as a treat.

I should mention that although the house was new to the Hawkins family, it wasn't no new house. In fact it was far from it. Folks called it a shotgun house, 'cause from the outside it looked like it got blasted with the business end of a semiautomatic rifle. I think there were three rooms total in the house: a living room, a kitchen, and a bedroom. Maybe there was two bedrooms, I don't rightly remember, but I do know that the kids slept crossways four to a bed and some on the floor when it wasn't too cold and some on a couch in the living room. There was no running water indoors, and only an outhouse, and to take a bath you heated water on the stove and poured it in a tin tub that you hung a curtain around. The living room was plastered with newspaper, and from inside the house you could look through the cracks in the walls and see the yard outside, and you could look down through the floor and see the dirt under the house. It gets mighty chilly in the winter in Montgomery, below freezing, and a wind will blow in December which makes things seem colder even still, and the house was heated only with a fireplace and a cooking stove. Mama cooked sweet potatoes in the fireplace because they baked better in there. Whatever Mama fixed is what everybody ate, and no matter what she fixed we was always full. We had a daddy who worked as hard as a man could and he wasn't going to allow his family to go hungry neither, and if this man let him down then he was going to go higher to the next man, and if that man let him down he was going to go higher to get his wages, and that hope of a better tomorrow was why we had moved to the city.

More kids came along and soon enough there was Willela and Alice and Henry and Edward to join the family, though if you hear me say Edward's name today I run it all close together, almost like *Etwud*, and he was to become one of my favorite brothers, probably the most favorite because he is so funny and kind and cool. That meant nine children for the Hawkins family by 1947. I think some of the four original uncle boys from Grandma's family had started to move out on their own then. Then Mama became pregnant again and this time it was with twins.

That's how I came to be. There was no money for the hospital— there never was—so a midwife came and she had a good reputation as folks say but maybe if Mama had been in the hospital they would have been able to save the other twin. The other baby was born with the cord wrapped around her neck and she soon passed and so the family had to bury her. They called her Mary Ann and they called me Martha Ann, like Mary and Martha the sisters of Lazarus, though we soon dropped the Ann from behind my name and I was just known as Martha from then on. I guess I wasn't much of a baby to look at, being underweight as the only surviving twin. I was sickly at first and I had something wrong with a kidney my Mama said, because things with me were never quite right in that area, and being the tenth child I guess it would have been easy for folks to think of me as just another mouth to feed but I know my mama and daddy welcomed me to the family because that's how they were. My oldest sister was eighteen years old by the time I came along and the children stretched out every other year or so until me. Mama and Daddy would have two more boys eventually, Tom and Howard, so it would make twelve children in all for the Hawkins family, plus my twin sister who died and two other stillborn babies that Mama had birthed along the years, so I guess we weren't much different from most big families I knew who stayed in our area.

As a kid I had short kinky hair and what I thought was a big space between my upper lip and my nose. I was big for my age too. I wasn't fat or even fluffy, just big boned with large hands and sturdy shoulders. One day my mama went to town to get new shoes. Normally we just wore flour sack dresses that Mama tore and sewed up again and whatever shoes was around if it was cold enough to need shoes, but this was a special occasion that called for a pair of new shoes. There was a shoe shop and a barbershop right next to each other. She was announcing to somebody at the shoe shop that one of her babies was getting married—one of the older girls, I don't remember who (that's who the new shoes was for)—and the lady she was talking to looked at me and said that I was the biggest baby she'd ever seen. It got a good guffaw out of all the fellas at the barbershop but I didn't smile. I can't ever remember a time that I received a compliment for being pretty as a child or having a nice smile.

Mostly I longed to be old enough so I could go to work with my sisters and brothers. It must have been summer because they was all out of school, and every day a big truck came by the neighborhood and they all clambered on to go somewhere and pick cotton. The truck picked them up at 4 A.M. every morning and they carried their lunches with them, riding on the back of the truck to the fields and coming back late in the evening. I couldn't wait until I got bigger so I could go pick cotton just like them—they looked like they were having so much fun. One day I asked my older sister Alice about it. "Girl, what's the matter with you?" she said. "Your hands get all blistered and you're all stuck with calluses. It's all sweaty out there. You must be crazy for wanting to pick cotton." That was the last of that question.

I had other questions though, as a child, and I dared to ask them when I could. I knew enough to pray and I did so whenever I felt inclined, which was quite a lot. God, if he was truly up there, seemed to listen really well. I knew they talked about God a lot in the church we went to every Sunday, but church always seemed such a place for catching hell. There was always a lot of shouting going on, such a lot of singing and screaming and crying and carrying on. Somebody was always wagging his finger at you at church, sweating and moaning and warning you to shape up and escape the eternal fires of damnation. I liked looking out at the stars at night instead. It was more peaceful having a conversation with God outside where it was just him and me and quiet.

One Christmas I thought church was pretty good though. It was good for what I took away from the preaching, whether it was intended to be taken that way or not, and this gets back to the questions I dared ask as a child. I knew it was Christmas because we had each gotten fruit as a present. I got an orange. That was all I got as a present that particular Christmas but I thought that orange was mighty fine, sweet and sticky, and the juice rolled down my chin and I laughed. I shared some of mine with Edward and he shared some of his apple with me. The only time during the year that we ever saw fruit was at Christmas. Years later I was so surprised to go to a grocery store and see that they had fruit available all twelve months of the year. But what you can't see you can't long for and then not get, at least that was Mama's theory.

Anyway, on this particular Christmas we bundled up and walked down to St. James #2 for the service, and the reverend was all shouting and preaching and sweating in December with his Bible flopped open in one hand and his finger wagging with the other, and I sat on a pew next to Edward thinking about the orange I had just ate and how good it was and looking at the rough box manger they had set up on the stage wishing it was filled with oranges when all of a sudden the preacher said something that made me start. He said, "No crying he made." The baby Jesus, he meant. He must have been quoting from that old Christmas song about the little Lord Jesus asleep on the hay, but something about it all didn't sound right with what I had experienced, young as I was. I thought: I know he's a preacher and all but I don't think the man's right this time. And I hoped it wasn't a sin to think that way. But I bet that the little Lord Jesus, if he was like any of the babies I had ever knowed, made a heap of crying. It was a new thought to me and I let it roll around in my mind as the preacher waggled on about the *incarnation* or some fancy word. I just figured that if God Almighty was indeed all that almighty then he could come to earth from heaven in any form he wanted to. He could have come as a rich man or the president of America or a plantation owner, for all that matter. But no, he came as a little baby. So I bet he did his coming-to-earth thing right, being God and truthful and all, and I bet he was screechy and filled his diaper with nappy messes and lay in that manger hay all flailing about with his tiny arms and legs, same as any baby I had ever seen lie in a wood box around our house.

Edward nudged me, and I noticed everybody was standing now. The choir to my left had flapped to their feet all wearing their robes, and they started swaying and singing high and shouty as a good gospel chorus does, and there was more clapping and carrying on, and then I wised up quick and stood in a hurry as to not get a smack from Mama later on and I started to sing and clap along with the rest of the congregation and choir. But I kept thinking as I stood and sang, and as I thought I asked a question of myself that would begin to stick in my craw like a piece of corn bread that needs some milk to go down. I asked myself: What sort of hope would a baby like that baby Jesus ever have in the world? I think it was the biggest question of my life to that point, but really it was a question I was asking of myself, though I may have not been able to phrase it in such a manner just then—for any baby born into such a predicament as that must have had its questioners, and I knowed that there are many born around the world into such predicaments just the same as Jesus. Most of the kids in my family and neighborhood that I knowed was born that way and that's how I felt my birth was like—similar to Jesus'. What hope would that child have? What life quality could Jesus ever possibly find and enjoy, born to a poor carpenter daddy and a teenage mama and not even married at first with Joseph all wanting to put Mary away quietly like the Bible said? What dreams would I one day ever strive to conjure and someday dare to realize when I was born to a bike-riding daddy who worked in a fertilizer factory and to a mama who took in laundry from neighbors and tended children? The thought was nothing against my mama and daddy, just a sudden realization of the humble place in life to which I was born. Here I was thrust upon the world as a poverty-stricken black girl born into a region where I was immediately dubbed as second class. There are some folks who would say a child such as this would have been better off not being born. I am sure of that, for I hear smatterings of such talk even today. There was little purpose for her life, some folks will argue. She was of faint consequence and not even particularly pretty to look at. What good was she? What good was Jesus, then? What hope did that tiny boy baby born in a stable ever have for doing something successful with his life?

The more I rolled the question around in my tiny brain, the more it made my neck hot. I knowed it bothered Edward too, for I tried to phrase it to him on the way home from church. "Girl, what kind of fool talk is that?" he said and pushed my shoulder. Not rough or mean like some kids did, for Edward was never that way, but just in a mad way, like maybe he was trying to roll around the question for himself and didn't want to. "We are as gooda folks as anybody around here," Edward said to me. "Look at what we just got for Christmas! You got an orange and I got an apple, and if that ain't as good as a gumdrop then I don't know what is!" He shoved me again for good measure, a little less hard this time, then started running down the dirt road toward home.

Mama would be cooking a Christmas dinner for us when we got there. There would be bacon and collards and a big pot of black-eyed peas simmering on the stove, though when Edward started to run I knowed without a doubt that he was wrestling with that question, for that's what that question does to people. I knowed that he must have heard folks imply such things about his birth too, in one such way or another. The bigger question was of our right to existence, and I knowed that any question such as that would raise a fury inside of Edward, for that's what it raised inside of me, although I could not articulate it for many years. And so I kept it locked tightly inside myself where it simmered, and not in a good way neither like that pot of peas on Mama's potbellied stove, but it simmered in a harmful way where it would come near to destroy me, this hurt, this great frustration of so little hope, and perhaps the fear of letting it boil over completely was why I kept it stuffed so deep inside me all that time.

Surely I knowed that my family loved me. That was my hope for the moment. We came back to the house and ate our Christmas feast and I never questioned that love for a minute. Daddy was always kind. Every day he brought me something home from his lunch he had saved for me. It might have been a piece of his sandwich or a slice of corn bread. Somehow he always brought me home an extra little bit of food as a treat, and whenever we walked anywhere together he held my hand. Mama was tougher. She was the disciplinarian in the family. She had a million lines for any child who got out of hand: "Don't you sass me. You need a whupping. Go fetch me a stick, child." Mama was always quick on the draw with a switch and certainly I feared that very thing when I was slow to stand in church. It didn't even matter if you was right; if Mama determined you needed a switching, then you received a switching. There was no jury. There was only one judge and she was Mama, and Mama's law was all that mattered. "Are you disputing me?" she said one day to me when I was sure I was right. "Are you disputing my words, child, because I ain't gonna say them again?" It was a phrase we would all hear. We might be right, but we got the switch anyway. Being right made no nevermind to Mama.

There was always people in our home. January, February, March—it didn't matter the month. That was also part of Mama and Daddy's love, part of the security they offered to us as children: they would always provide—for us, for anyone. We never doubted it, though sometimes we worried it. Most times I knew the folks who ate with us, sometimes I didn't. Regularly people from the neighborhood stopped by to eat and Mama always fed them. I don't know how she did it but there was always enough. She threw some more peas in the pot or added more water and salt. Somehow people always ate and ate and ate. I loved watching Mama cook and I helped whenever she let me. Her making soda biscuits was the best. They was always baked in big portions so there'd be enough, lightly browned but never hardened on the outside. They were moist and light with soft, fine-grained crumbs, flaky and tender and warm, and piled with country butter. Anybody who came to the house was welcome to eat those biscuits. That's when Mama was at her best, when she was cooking, feeding, having company around.

Everybody always talked around the supper table. Even us kids. That was part of the love too. You were welcome to talk, and everybody all talked at once, often all at the same time. Talking was not about listening so much as about having fun talking. Somebody would spin a story and that would set somebody else off and she would tell another story and everybody would laugh and slap their knees and that would remind somebody else about a time where something else funny happened, and so it went on and on. We talked a lot in our family for sure, but we was never a family for talking about how we truly felt about nothing. We was a family who was busy with going to school and work and putting food on the table, and there wasn't much room for talking about feelings in a family like that. Not back then anyway, though we do much more of it today.

This sounds strange to say in a house of so many people, but it was easy for me to feel alone a lot as a child. There was two boys beneath me in age and two boys above me and my nearest sister Alice was seven years away. Georgia, Rosalee, and Alberta were already teenagers by the time I was born. Willela was nine. So it was mostly me and the four younger boys, Henry, Edward, Tom, and Howard. A lot of times I felt like the only girl in the family. I don't ever remember asking my older sisters for advice about anything, though they probably would have answered something if I had.

One day I was outside playing ball with my brothers, which I often did. Some neighborhood kid got his nose out of joint and jumped on Edward and started to wale on him. Well, Edward was two years older than me and could surely take care of himself, but this neighborhood boy was known a bully and Edward was my favorite brother. So I jumped on the bully's back and started waling on him to help out Edward. The bully tossed me off in the dust so I went and got a stick and whacked him across the thigh as hard as I could. He shouted filth and foul and let go of Edward. This gave my brother enough time to spin around, face his assailant, and land a few quick haymakers upside the bully's jaw. The bully yelped louder and ran off down the street. Edward looked at me and grinned. That was the last of that. Ain't nobody was going to be messing with my brother. Edward was going to look out for me, and I was going to look out for him. That was our plan for dealing with the world.

When we got home later that afternoon, Daddy was already there though it was half an hour still to go in the workday. A man had come by and told him that Progress was coming through the neighborhood. They was building a big road right smack near our backyard and we all had to move. Most all the neighbors needed to. The man didn't give us noplace to go. Certainly no money to help in moving. We were out on our ears. Daddy had been out looking for a new place to live but it was tough going to find a place we could afford. I had never seen Daddy look worried before, or seen a look that I could identify as such anyway. But that day his eyebrows were set together in a new way. "They's always pushing people around," Daddy said. "That's what the man does. He tells us what we can do and what we can't. Somebody's always telling us what we can and can't do." He was getting tired of being pushed around, I knew that much for sure.

That was all Daddy said for a spell. He went out again early that evening to look for a new place his family could stay. Mama went with him this time. Edward and I went outside and began to toss a ball back and forth on the dirt in the front yard. I could see Edward's heart wasn't in the game because he missed a few of my throws and he never did that before.

"Where do you think we're going to move to?" I asked him after a time.

"I don't know, girl," he said. His eyes were far away, like he was still thinking about that bigger question I had asked him once. "I don't know where we're going to all end up. But I'm sure Mama and Daddy will figure it out soon."

I tried to smile to encourage Edward. "They gots to, Edward. I know they will."

Edward tossed me the ball. He nodded. "Let's go inside for the night, girl," he said. "I'm beginning to feel a chill."

3

Our Heaven in the Projects

I LOOKED INTO EDWARD'S EYES. They was round as cake pans. I'm sure mine was too. He was looking back at me, his mouth hanging open, and we turned from looking at each other and looked back at the toilet again—its cold porcelain exterior gleamed in the early evening sunlight, its shiny metal handle caught the glow and beamed rays around the room. Edward examined the lid in the down position then lifted it and examined the insides then set it down again carefully so as to not upset the balance of wonder.

"It must stink," I said in a hushed tone. I wasn't letting myself get too carried away for fear of disappointment. "Whoever heard of putting such a thing indoors?" Surely this marvelous setup was too good to be true.

"Don't talk foolish, girl," Edward said. "They gots these nowadays in the city. City folks don't put up with no such nonsense as stink."

"How are you gonna be sure?" I asked. "I'm worried it will stink up the place." I was thinking about the odors that wafted from our outhouse back at the North Montgomery house. Edward was not one to be mistrusted, but I was full of questions this day because we had just moved into our new apartment at the corner of North Bainbridge and Randolph streets, and all was new. A sign out front read TRENHOLM COURT and lots of folks were to stay there alongside us. It was part of the new housing projects that Daddy said was giving folks a hand up. It was okay to accept help from the public housing authority if the hand helped you go forward, Daddy said, but if the hand that helped you kept you stuck then it wasn't no use and you wasn't to take it. The Hawkins family was going forward, Daddy insisted, and besides there wasn't no other place to go that we could afford, so that's how we came to stay at Trenholm Court on the other side of the railroad tracks from where we used to live before Progress came through in North Montgomery.

"Go on," Edward said. "Try it out. I'll close the door behind me and leave. You'll see for yourself it don't stink."

"I don't have to go just now," I said. It was no lie. I was keeping everything locked tight within me, even the excitement I was feeling about everything new. Edward didn't have to go neither so we just kept letting our eyes wander all over that new toilet inside our new bathroom. Next to that toilet was a new glossy tub that had real running water that you didn't have to heat on top of a stove first. We turned the handles on that tub and oohed and aahed over the water's gush while imagining ourselves getting clean in it. It was the first real indoor tub the Hawkins family had ever called its own. There was a new polished plate mirror that hung on the wall too. Yes sir, that Trenholm Court had everything.

"C'mon," Edward said. "We can look at the toilet again later on. Let's go exploring." We headed out from the bathroom, passing Mama who was already in the kitchen. She was fixing corn bread and pork chop casserole for dinner. Edward and I ran through our tiny yard to where our little red wagon was parked at the yard's edge. He nodded and pointed with his head. "Hop in and I'll pull you," he said. I obliged and Edward began to pull me on down the road.

Each building in Trenholm Court looked just like the other. They were low, flat redbrick buildings joined to each other in rows, sort of like the military housing apartments that I had seen pictures of once. Each front door in Trenholm Court had a small cement slab that acted as a porch. Each front yard had a big metal T-shaped pole to act as a clothes drier, and lines of laundry fluttered as far as I could see. There was plenty of kids playing in every yard, and some had a base-ball game going a couple of apartments away, and a group of older boys with pressed slacks and white T-shirts and fedoras were hanging out all cool by a Dumpster. One musta had his own transistor radio because there was music buzzing from a little green box with a yel-low dial and I recognized the piano solo from "Mess Around" by Ray Charles and some of the lyrics. It was a big hit in 1953. We stayed in number 464, an end unit, and Daddy had already erected a short fence around our yard to close us in from the street. There wasn't no grass in our yard, just red dirt like there was in every yard, but I had heard Mama talking about how she was going to plant flowers soon by the front door and make things pretty.

Edward and I were already some distance from our apartment now. We was still on Union Circle, the name of the road that ran through the middle of the projects, but it didn't feel like we was heading the same direction as before. The sun looked different and it had almost set. We passed by a park with some swings and teeter-totters set up on the dirt. There was more kids and more redbrick row houses and everything looked the same as it did on our side of the projects.

"Hey Edward, just where are we anyway?" I asked.

"We're exploring," he said with that grin of his. "And I don't rightly know where we are. But if we just keep walking I'm sure we'll come to someplace." He shook his head then changed the subject. "What do you want to be when you grow up anyway?"

"A fighter just like Joe Lewis," I said. It was the first thing that popped into my fool head and I said it too quickly because Edward laughed at me until I thought he would drop. He smacked me on the side of my shoulder where I sat in the red wagon.

"Ain't no ways you'll ever be a boxer. They don't lets girls do that. Girls ain't never gonna be boxers. You know that."

I felt my face growing hot. "I was just kidding. What you gonna be, Edward?"

"Probably I'll go into the military. They pays for you to be whatever you wants to be. After that I'm going to be a fireman and save people."

The military. Did other folks actually pay for your education? I was only six but I knowed that we didn't have no money for book learning of much sorts. I was thinking fast. "Hey that sounds good to me, Edward," I announced, "I'm going to go into the military too." Then I pulled back and swallowed. "Do they let girls in the military, Edward?" I wanted to make sure. I didn't know what I'd do either when I got out of the military, but I was sure it would be something important.

"Yessa they do," he said. "That might be a real good place for you, Martha." He craned his neck around at me. Edward was always reading and he knowed everything. "I heard they gots a program called the WAC—Women's Army Corps it stands for. Had it since World War II. You could go into that, girl. You do that and be whatever you wanna be."

I smiled all my teeth. I could've hugged Edward for believing in me like that. We was both silent for a bit as we kept moving through the court. The sun was just about down now but its glow looked like it was in the wrong spot in the sky. It was getting a mite chilly too.

"You sure you knows where we are, Edward?" I asked. His neck muscles tensed up and he hunched his shoulders and pulled the wagon a bit quicker. "I ain't ever seen none of this before." The wagon jostled over a rock in the dirt and slid me over and down with a little jolt.

He was quiet for about twenty more feet, then said at last, "I thinks we lost, Martha." He said it quietly as if not to scare me. He was only eight. Then he gave a little check and began to jog, still pulling the handle.

Lost? I didn't like the sound of that word at all. How was we ever gonna get home? I held on to the sides of the wagon as it lurched across the gravel. Union Court seemed to flow in a big circle of a street. This was all a new neighborhood to us. I wasn't sure which direction we was headed now. Edward was sweating. He increased his pace. The wagon flew along. I was scared I'd fall out and I could feel my insides tighten even further. I really had to use that new bathroom of ours now. We rattled along the dirt street in a rush. I hated that feeling of having lost my bearings. Lord knows I would feel it more than once in my life.

Suddenly Edward slowed. He had caught sight of the same Dumpster, the same familiar lines of laundry. Union Circle wound all the way through the court. We had come out the other side and were right back where we started. I gushed out air through my mouth in relief. Daddy was standing at the edge of our yard with his hand shading his eyes when we came up. "I was just starting to get worried about y'all," he said. "Hurry inside now. Your mama's got supper on."

Warm smells filled my nose as we walked in. The kitchen was all lighted and there was familiar pots steaming on the stove. Mama and my older sisters were bustling about getting dishes and spoons ready. I ran to the indoor bathroom and enjoyed a sit-down, then washed my hands with real running water from the tap as Mama had taught me and headed for the supper table. The pork chop casserole was piled high on a serving bowl in the middle. A plate of fresh corn bread was sliced and steaming on a platter to one side. There was a slab of good country butter, and tall glasses of milk were set by every plate, the glasses already beaded with little wet bubbles on the outsides. We sat—Mama and Daddy and Edward and me and my sisters and brothers and Daddy's great-aunt, Mom Rose we called her, who had come to live with us and was the only grandma I ever knowed, and my sister who was already married and her two girls, who had also come to live with us. We all held hands and bowed our heads and Daddy prayed a thanksgiving over the meal and we all dived in and began to eat. I settled back as Daddy spooned my plate high with the good casserole and I took the first bite and it felt like all the comfort of being where I was supposed to be. The casserole was salty and smooth from the butter and just about too hot to eat but I blew on my spoon and it went down my throat and made me feel happy inside. All of a sudden, in that very same moment, I knew what I wanted to do with my life. Whenever I got out of the military and got my education or whatever I would get with the WAC I would make a place that felt just like this supper table. I would open a place where people could eat and I'd serve people comfort food like the pork chop casserole we was having tonight. It wouldn't be no ordinary restaurant neither. When people was out getting lost wandering around Union Circle or doing whatever people do to feel tight inside and worried that they might never find their way home, I would tell 'em to come into my restaurant, and they would feel like they had come home at last. Their mama would be cooking in that restaurant, or someone who seemed just like their mama to them, anyway. And they would sit next to friendly people they knowed, and grace would be prayed over their supper if they was praying folks, and they would settle in and give a big sigh and they would know that when they was eating supper in my restaurant that they had come home for sure. That's what I would do. I knowed it right there like I knowed it for sure. I would open a restaurant someday and give people little slices of all that was good.

After dinner Daddy put on a record in the living room. We had an old record player that you wound up. Daddy put on Nat King

Cole, who wasn't fast enough for my liking, but Mister King Cole came on with his smooth voice and scratched sound over the turntable and we waltzed around the room as he sang. Then Alice put on one she liked by Big Mama Thornton, and she cranked the volume as she cranked the record player, and now we all danced and hooted and hollered all around the living room. We was all dancing then. All except Alice, who was cranking the recorder, and Mama, who said she didn't feel like it just then. We shook and shimmied and swung our arms and shook our behinds. Here we were the Hawkins family living in our new digs in Trenholm Court. We was living in the projects and it was heaven for me. Real heaven. I wished that night could have gone on forever.

4

Different

TRENHOLM COURT MEANT GOING TO school. On my first day walking to W. B. Paterson Elementary I kept to myself and didn't say much, although all the kids from the neighborhood walked the quarter mile or so up the hill together for school and that felt like fun to me. Edward walked beside me. Henry was in his last year at that school, and all my other brothers and sisters were older than that and went elsewhere, if they was still in school then. Edward and me walked by the little corner store on South Bainbridge Street. It was owned by Mister Jakes, a man with a craggy nose and a hairy chin, and Mama sent us over to his store all the time to get a half pound of sugar or this or that. He had a couple of kids about my age or just a little older, and as Edward and I walked by I noticed like they was getting ready to go to school with their faces all pink and ruddy in the September morning so I waved and smiled but Edward pulled my hand back real quick like. "They don't go to our school," he hissed. "You don't wave at them, Martha."

All the kids at W. B. Paterson were black. That's how it was. White kids went someplace else. My school was for grades one through six, no kindergarten and no gymnasium, no buses or sports, and certainly no such thing as a music or art program, but it had a row of shady trees near the parking lot and a library and a big yard outside where we could play during recess and lunch. Across the street was a big old cemetery with a heap of gravestones that looked like little boxes scattered around the hillside. The great honky-tonk singer Hank Williams had died the year before in 1953, and somebody said he was buried in that cemetery but I didn't know much about honky-tonk, although Mister Williams had begun his career years earlier in Montgomery and I was proud of our city for giving rise to somebody as famous as that.

All the kids dressed pretty much the same at W. B. Paterson. Boys wore pants or overalls and flannel shirts, girls wore simple cotton dresses. Most kids I knowed didn't wear shoes except in winter months when you hads to have them. Everybody was scrubbed shiny by their mamas, yet every kid sort of looked frayed around the edges too. We got books at school, they passed them out on the first day—real books, and plenty of them. I got a science book from the 1920s, and a math book from about the same year, and a reader about two kids named Dick and Jane. The cover of my reader was torn off but I looked at the girl's next to me and on the front cover of hers I could see Jane wearing a pink dress and her blond curls bounced up and down as she ran and Dick wore khaki shorts and a blue short-sleeved shirt and they were heading somewhere mighty quick and smiling. "They always give us the raggedy books," Edward said at lunch when I asked him about my torn cover. "Don't you know nothing, Martha? They pass out the new books at the school where Mister Jakes's kids go. They give those kids the books first.

Then when they're done reading them they give them to us and those kids get new ones." I wanted to ask why, but the look on Edward's face made me not want to ask any more questions just then.

I didn't know much about that big word I heard Daddy say: *segregation*. Kids was just kids to me. The only swimming pool in Montgomery was across town in Oak Park and we coloreds wasn't allowed in Oak Park at all. We had just heard you could swim there but none of us actually knew how to swim much so it wasn't no nevermind to us. There was a movie theater downtown that we were allowed to go to but it was full of rats so we hardly never went. It cost money too for a bus fare and a movie ticket, so that was something to stop us also.

We didn't get out where the whites were much. We were isolated at Trenholm Court, isolated in our communities of people colored just like us. My brother Henry got a job as a caddy on Saturdays and Sundays at the golf course. Blacks couldn't go there except to work. One day my brother got angry because someone called him a name. The man paying for golf said, "Hey, come here, Sunflower." So Henry got angry and dumped the man's caddy bag and left. He came home and told Daddy that he lost his job at the golf course. Jobs were hard to come by but Daddy didn't get upset. He was happy that Henry had stood up for himself. He called us all over, all of us who were home anyway, and said that something had happened that year, 1954, where there was a court case called *Brown v. the Board of Education* that said that black kids and white kids didn't have to go to separate schools no more. I didn't know much about that because the lawsuit had been filed way up in Kansas and Daddy said it would be a while before things in Alabama changed, but he said that new winds of hope were blowing all across this country, and things would be different for our generation he was sure. That sounded fine to me. Daddy knew what it had been like more than we did. I just hoped that maybe soon I would get a new reader, one with Dick and Jane still on the cover. And maybe soon I could wave to those white kids of Mister Jakes who owned the corner store when they was going to school. Maybe we'd even go to the same school and be friends. I could always use more friends.

A year later in 1955 there was a woman who lived in our city named Rosa Parks. Daddy told me the story when he came home from work one day. He said the man was always changing the ways that coloreds could sit on the buses, and this woman, Missus Parks, she didn't want to change seats after a while. So she kept sitting down when a white man got on the bus and wanted to sit in her seat and so they arrested her. Then all the folks in Montgomery got together and said they wasn't going to ride the buses no more in protest of Rosa Parks getting thrown into jail. I didn't ride city buses much, but Mama did whenever she needed to go downtown. There was a bus stop right on the corner of Trenholm Court. So for some time after that she walked wherever she went or rode Daddy's bike when he wasn't using it. That bus boycott ended up lasting a whole year and cost the bus company a heap of money. It was never no good to cost a company money, Daddy said, but it made the man stand up and take a look at what was going on. In the end the Alabama state court said that from now on whites and coloreds could ride the same buses and coloreds could sit wherever we wanted to. That sounded good, though it didn't much matter to me as a child.

There was an organization that met over in West Montgomery at the Holt Street Baptist Church. It was called the Montgomery Improvement Association, or the MIA for short. In the years that followed we could go up there anytime we wanted to go to an MIA meeting. Sometimes it met at the church, and sometimes it met on South Jackson Street at the Ben Moore Hotel with the Majestic Café underneath. Daddy said it was good for us to attend. We was all learning how to be free, he said. I didn't quite all understand that but I knowed that whenever I walked downtown with Mama that any restaurant we passed had two water fountains, one for whites and one for coloreds. The one for coloreds was always grubby and you never wanted to stick your face down close to the spigot even though it got real hot outside and you were sweating of thirst. And

H. L. Green, a five-and-dime store chain that we went to, had two lunch counters and the bigger one was for whites and it had chairs and tables where folks could sit down if they wanted, but the one for coloreds was smaller and we had to stand. I knowed, because I had seen it and I had stood there. And the bus station for going out of town had a separate door for whites to walk through and another door for blacks. There was two waiting rooms there also, and the waiting room was nicer for the whites. I had seen a doctor's office a few times. The one we went to had chairs for blacks but the chairs were hard and had no cushions. The chairs for whites had cushions. I wondered how it felt to be sitting on those cushions when I could see those cushions plain as day like that. And we knew there was folks coming in to the doctor's office with appointments later than us, but if they were white then they got to go ahead of us in line. Us blacks always had to wait longer for everything. It was just the way it was.

I wasn't sure about all the ins and outs of being free, but I had a few hopes for myself. Mostly I wondered if when they stopped segregation they could do something about stopping my principal's paddle. That was the kind of freedom I hoped for. They called her Missus Oglethorpe and she was fat and she loved her paddle, yes sir she rightly did. One morning me and my younger brothers, Tom and Howard, were walking up to school and the bell hadn't rung yet. It was time to go inside but three teachers was at the back door and said we couldn't go in, that we had to go around to the other door. We knew if we took the time to run around to the other door we'd be late by then and Missus Oglethorpe would give us her paddle. But we also knew better than to argue with teachers so I said okay and we left, but as soon as we were out of sight I said, "Let's go home" to Tom and Howard, and they thought that sounded mighty fine so we ditched school and walked home.

"What's going on?" Mama wanted to know when we showed up at home again.

"Ain't no school today," I said. It was a barefaced lie and we all knew it. Then to make matters worse Tom gave a little start and Howard's suddenly got the hiccups or something and old Missus Oglethorpe can be seen swinging her arms down the road toward us. She's got the fury of hell at her back and she marched up to us and wanted to know why we ain't at school. I tried to say something about the teachers at the door but I knowed it was gonna be useless to try and explain that logic to a grown-up, particularly a grown-up who's holding a paddle and is itching to swing it in our backsides' direction, so I just kept my mouth shut and looked at the dirt. That throwed a wrench in Missus Oglethorpe's plan, for she appeared as if she wanted some sort of explanation from me. She was throwing sweat beads off her forehead now, she was so mad, so finally she just said, "Well, you children need a whupping." Mama was no fool and had seen through our plan by now and agreed. Missus Oglethorpe offered to do the whupping right there on the spot but Mama said that they were her children and she'd do the job thank you. We were not allowed to return to school that day as punishment, which sounded fine to us although we didn't say nothing. I don't know what influenced Mama—it musta been the heaven of living in the projects rubbing off on her—but Mama plumb forgot about that whupping. Or maybe she was getting softer on whuppings as the years were passing by. Perhaps she knew that sometimes a kid has got enough whuppings for a while, but she never gave us one just then.

The next morning at school Missus Oglethorpe marched over to us and asked us if our Mama had whupped us.

"Yessum," I said. "We was thoroughly whupped through and through by our mama." It was a lie, of course, but what was I going to say? That our mama hadn't whupped us? That would have been the real tragedy of the whole goings-on. Some people just treat you better than others, no matter what their color, I think that's what I learned from that experience. Missus Oglethorpe was black and I didn't like her much, but I had some other good teachers at W. B. Paterson. Miss Walker taught fourth grade and she was a real peach.

Miss Clayton taught me sixth grade and I just loved her. They were happy teachers who loved teaching, and they made all the difference, no matter what school we was in.

In my early teen years I went to a different school, Booker T. Washington, for seventh and eighth grades. It was about three miles from my house and all us kids from Trenholm Court walked there and back. About that time everything in the city seemed to heat up more and more as well. Daddy kept us up on all the news reports. A colored truck driver named Willie Edwards Jr. had been on his way to work in Montgomery when he was stopped by four Klansmen. The Klansmen mistook Willie Edwards for another colored man they thought was dating a white woman. They didn't care for that much so they pulled their guns and forced Willie Edwards to jump off a bridge into the Alabama River where he drowned. I felt sad for poor old Willie Edwards. That was the river that ran right by our old house in North Montgomery.

Several times Daddy took us to hear Martin Luther King Jr. speak. He was the pastor of a little redbrick church in downtown Montgomery called the Dexter Avenue Baptist Church. I had seen the church building once or twice and it wasn't much to look at. What was impressive about Mister King's church was that it sat only about a block away from the Alabama State Capitol building. Here was this funny little church building with its white porches and wooden belfry and then sprawled a block away was this huge stone building with its glassy dome on top and piles of steps to the front doors and huge Greek pillars holding it all up. It was like the humble and the powerful was lying down next to each other side by side. And, my, how that preacher could preach. Reverend King's voice ebbed and flowed and he talked about change coming and the birth of a new nation and about souls who were crying for freedom and about how there was a great day ahead. I liked to hear him talk. Rumor was that they was holding meetings at Dexter Avenue Baptist for all the "movement" leaders, as they were starting to call it. I was sad when Daddy told us the parsonage at Dexter Avenue got bombed but I was glad to hear that Mrs. King and her pretty daughter Yolanda weren't hurt.

We'd been joining some of the MIA marches and our marches with the MIA became more frequent. One evening we headed up the hill to the Baptist church, it was still light outside, and they organized us into this big march. Then we started heading down the hill toward the city talking about what it meant to have hope ahead, and some folks were singing songs as they walked, and things was just peaceful although there was a sense of expectancy with the crowd. Over yonder I heard a scream let out. There was maybe a hundred or so folks marching and it's hard to say exactly what happened in the next few minutes because things were all dusty real sudden against the sky. I heard horses galloping and whinnying and lots of people were shouting and screaming now. Some men with white sheets over their heads were swinging toward us at a full gallop. They had eyeholes cut in their sheets so they could see and some had capes on that were streaming out behind them. The folks on horses had whips and started busting the marchers with those whips. It didn't matter who it was or if you were a boy or girl, the whips busted down over and over. I heard them sizzle and zap, sizzle and zap. Folks were screaming now everywhere, all of us frenzied to get away. I sprinted as hard as I could in the only direction that made sense to me: I ran for home. Over to my right I saw a girl get run over and stepped on by a horse. It didn't look like the man riding the horse made no effort to turn his horse, he just plowed right into the girl and kept galloping over her. The girl screamed and looked mighty broke up and I wanted to help her but there was a press of folks between me and her and so I kept running. There was maybe twenty men on horses and whipping us marchers and everybody was trying so desperate to get away. Then some colored fella swung up behind one of the Klansmen and caught the man's hood and ripped it off. Underneath I gasped to see the same craggy nose and hairy chin of Mister Jakes. This was the same man whose store we always went to. We had seen his kids working in the store and I wanted to wave to his kids that morning on the way to school but Edward said no. That was a shocker: our very own neighbor was a Klansman.

The march was over real quick that night. A day later somebody came by the house and said that Mister Jakes's store had been broken up after the march. The thought was that we had caught him wrong. He was living in our neighborhood and would certainly take our money, but when it came to marching then he would be out on a horse running over us with a whip. We had supported his business all these years, all the colored folks in the neighborhood had, so the belief was that he deserved some retaliation and they had busted up his store real good. Daddy never shook his head at this, one way or another. When he heard this news he called us to him and pressed us against his side more tightly and told us that things were afoot now and that we needed to be more careful than we usually were. We all did.

I was at school when I heard that our apartment was burning. I know for certain it wasn't because of race because when I ran home with Edward, Tom, and Howard, we found all our belongings outside on the lawn. The firemen were there and they had hosed down the inside of our place real good. Mama was at the hospital with a burn on her arm. She had aimed to save the baby and had gotten him out. He wasn't a baby really. He was two years old and the son of my older sister. He had been playing with matches and got trapped behind the bed, and the bed caught on fire. Mama's arm got burned real bad and my nephew got third-degree burns on his face and lost some of his fingers. It felt scary to come home when home was all burned up like that. Daddy began to mop up and he called for us to do the same. There was lots of water damage in the apartment. Clothes and mattresses and furniture was all wet and smoky. There was nowhere else for us to go. Where could we go? We mopped up as best we could and kept living there.

My nephew stayed in the hospital a couple months, then came back to live with us. He was all bandaged up, his face, his arms.

When the bandages came off you could see the scars. Part of his face was smooth, and part was all skin grafts from his hips.

This was our life in the projects. I guess you could say it wasn't quite the heaven I had hoped it would be. But all that would change as soon as I met Reuben.

5

Ugly, Stupid

I WAS ALL SHOOK UP.

All the girls in my class were jumping and hollering right next to me and we was squealing and hugging each other. They couldn't believe it and I couldn't believe it neither. I knew I had been nominated, but when the school loudspeaker boomed out my name after lunchtime I thought I would plumb fall over and faint. *Martha Hawkins—eighth-grade homecoming queen.* My oh my, how that had a good ring to it.

Booker T. Washington School went up to twelfth grade, and I was a lowly eighth grader, not even a freshman yet by high school standards. Some girl in twelfth grade got picked as homecoming queen over the whole court, then each class picked its own separate class queen to ride in the car alongside her. That was what I was picked to be. The class queen position was picked by the classmates in your grade. When I thought about it that carried some weight to it. It meant a whole lot of people in eighth grade considered me . . . *Wait a minute . . . Could it actually be? . . .* They thought I was pretty!

Me?

I remembered the year before when I was twelve and had hit puberty. Nobody told me what all the bleeding was for but I figured how to take care of things in time. Now as a thirteen-year-old I was built up real nice with a low little waistline and my chest had come in. Grown men was always trying to talk to me, which I never did understand. Whenever I looked in the mirror I never thought I was much to look at. I still saw a nappy-headed kid with large bones and a big upper lip.

Being class homecoming queen meant I was to ride in a convertible on homecoming night in a parade. I was so excited I could barely sit still in class the next day. Mama and Willela helped me pick out a new dress for the evening. I don't know where the money for my new dress came from but Daddy said the money was there when it was needed. My dress was white chiffon with little straps and a shawl for my shoulders. I felt so pretty when I wore that dress in the department store. I looked in the full-length mirror and it was almost a real homecoming queen staring back at me.

The morning of homecoming I looked outside and saw rain. It was flowing down my window in Trenholm Court in buckets. It never rained in Montgomery. Why did it have to rain today? By lunchtime it slowed to a shower, but by early afternoon it turned into a regular downpour again. It rained and rained and rained. It rained all that day of the parade. I tried to pray but it seemed foolish to ask God for a miracle as unimportant as that. Sure enough the homecoming parade was canceled. That meant I didn't get to ride in the car or dress up in my gown even though Willela had fixed up my hair in curls because she was still hoping the rain would stop. Of course they still played football. Nothing stopped football. They played football in the mud and the grass and the boys ran up and down the field until you couldn't see nobody's uniform because of the muck. That was homecoming that year. Edward took me to the football game and we sat in the stands with Edward cheering for our Booker T. and me being more quiet because I didn't feel much like cheering just then. Edward took me to the homecoming game because I didn't have no date. What boy would ever ask ask me out? At least that's how I felt.

A year went by and I was in ninth grade, and that's when Edward's friend Reuben told Edward that he wanted to meet me at a basketball game. Reuben was a senior and it confused me why a senior like Reuben would want to talk to a freshman. Still, I felt good about it. I felt real good, actually. Whatever a senior like Reuben wanted, that was fine by me. Maybe this boy would actually like me. Maybe he would want to hold my hand as we walked across campus at school, just as I had seen my friends do with their boyfriends. That's what I dared hope for: a boy to hold my hand.

Sure enough Reuben did hold my hand after that basketball game, and sure enough he did want to kiss me. And I didn't say no. And later the next evening he went to my daddy and asked him if he could talk with him. Daddy sat in his chair in the living room and Reuben went inside and said hey, then he forgot why he came over and said maybe he could swing on by the next evening if it wasn't too much trouble. Daddy said okay. Reuben lived about two miles over in another housing project called Tulane Court. Sure enough the next evening he came over to talk to my daddy again. Reuben mustered up more courage this time I guess, because he told my daddy he thought I was real nice and he wondered, if it wouldn't be too much trouble or nothing, uh, sir, if he could ask me out on a date.

Daddy didn't say yes to Reuben right away. I was always secretly happy about that, although I never told my daddy how I felt. Daddy asked Reuben questions first before he said yes: where he lived, who his parents were, how he was doing in school, what he hoped he'd do one day . . . things like that. Reuben stared at the floor and tried to meet Daddy's level gaze and answered yes sir and no sir in all the right places. So just like that Reuben and me was dating.

I felt mighty fine about this. I truly did. It was a fine thing as a freshman girl to be dating a senior boy. And I liked Reuben, I genuinely did. It weren't no fireworks exactly, but he was nice and a sharp dresser and he could make me laugh whenever he clowned around. And he clowned a lot. We never went anyplace on our dates like the movies or anything. That cost money and there was none of that. Reuben just sat down and talked with me or we went to his mama's house at Tulane. I liked his mama and daddy real fine. They was kind to me. Some time went by and Reuben graduated and I was in tenth grade and Reuben was wondering what he might do.

I didn't know much about much. Reuben kissed me sometimes and I liked how that felt but he would get that look in his eyes like he wanted something more and I didn't know what to think about that. There wasn't no education about that in school or in the family. My parents sure didn't talk about nothing pertaining to that subject. My closest sister was seven years older than me and I didn't talk about that with her neither. We weren't raised up talking or sharing about things like that. You just didn't talk about that. You didn't.

One night in March of my sophomore year Reuben and me was upstairs at his mama's house. We had been alone in his bedroom before and mostly we just talked or kissed and it was never more than that, but that night he told me that things was changing and he was going into the service. He had signed up already and got his orders even and he was soon leaving for an air base in Mississippi so it was good-bye then.

I didn't want Reuben to go. I liked having him around. I got a little teary and hugged him and then he hugged me back and then he kissed me and from then on it was Reuben taking the lead. He told me I was beautiful and I didn't believe him, although it sent me spinning when he said that. He looked deep into my eyes and whispered that we didn't need to break up, that he would soon be coming back to Montgomery on leave and he'd be with me then and things would be the way they always were. I liked the sound of that. His voice got low and whispery and I had to ask him to repeat what he said. So he said it again and sure enough Reuben was telling me that he loved me. He really was. So I whispered those same words to him because I figured that's what you did at a time like that. There was more kissing then and his hands were all over me now and I let him do that though I knowed it was a sin, but I just wasn't thinking no more. He was going into the service and I was busy trying to please him because I was always trying to please somebody and he was making more moves by then and I was caught in the moment and I didn't want to say no for fear this boy wouldn't like me no more.

When it was all over we put on our clothes and I didn't feel good about it but Reuben was laughing and talking like it was nothing at all. Then he walked me home to my mama's house. Reuben was the first boy I had ever been with like that.

That was March when I was fifteen years old. I had no sense of how babies were made. April went by and I didn't get my period and I knew something wasn't right and then May went by and I missed my period again. That was two months now. You know how you're talking to friends at school and you say, well I got this friend who's got this problem, see, but you're really talking about yourself? Well I talked to some friends at school and that's how I found out I was in trouble. I told Reuben I was in trouble and he didn't seem surprised and said he'd talk to my mama for me and she'd know what to do.

We took a walk in Trenholm Court, the three of us, Reuben, Mama, and me, but it was just Reuben and Mama doing the talking. I wasn't a part of the conversation. I wanted to leave town, to go someplace where I was all alone. I just wished I had someplace to go. Mama said the news was no surprise to her because she had noticed I was wanting more biscuits and grits for breakfast lately. I wasn't sick in the mornings like my girlfriends said might happen, but Mama had given birth to a lot of children so she was no fool about a pregnancy when she saw one.

"So then it's settled," I heard Mama say. Her voice was matter-of-fact. "There'll be a wedding."

"Yessum," Reuben said. "I want to do the right thing, ma'am. I really do. I want to marry your daughter."

Just like that Reuben and I was engaged. I wasn't happy. I felt stuck. What did I know about having a husband or kids? I didn't want to get married, but what could I do? I talked to some friends at school again and a girl said she had heard that her cousin had got rid of a baby by jumping down a hill. After school that day I climbed up Houston Hill by my school and rolled down as hard as I could and then I tried it again with a little more jump, but it didn't do nothing. A miscarriage was one thing because it was natural, but an abortion wasn't nothing I wanted. Even if I did, who was I gonna talk to about that? That was something that wasn't talked about in my house neither. How could it have been with Mama having all those kids?

So I started to go through with plans for the wedding, and in late May I went to the doctor because I was told you was supposed to have a blood test before getting married. When the doctor came out from taking the test he had a grave look on his face. I didn't even know the word he was saying to me, and I didn't have no symptoms at all from the list he read me, but he said it was common not to have any symptoms and he wrote the word down on a piece of paper and explained it to me and asked a lot more questions:

Was I having relations with a lot of boys?

No sir, not at all. Only one. Reuben. And only once.

Was he having relations with a lot of girls?

Not that I knowed, sir. We didn't talk about it, but I was his girlfriend. I knowed that for sure.

Did he have any open sores that I knew of?

No sir. None that I'd ever seen.

Was he on a ship?

No sir.

Was he in the military?

Yes sir. He was in the military.

So he's been away for extended periods of time?

Well sir, he just went into the military, so I don't know.

You don't know where he's been before? Does he ever talk about dating other girls? Or about visiting brothels?

No sir. He doesn't talk about that.

Of course not, the doctor said. Of course not. But have your boyfriend come and see me. In the meantime you need to come back and take three shots. It'll clear up soon.

Reuben and me was supposed to get married June 7, but because the syphilis needed time to clear up Reuben moved the wedding back to June 30. That was the day of my sixteenth birthday. Reuben knew. Of course I had contracted the syphilis from him. He hemmed and hawed and said he had fallen and hurt his back and so he needed to move the wedding day later so his back would feel better. We couldn't talk about the truth. I was so mad at Reuben. Mad, or hurt, or maybe just disappointed—sometimes it was hard to identify what I was feeling. Why didn't he tell me he was having relations with other girls? I thought he loved me like I was the only girl for him.

Soon I dropped out of high school because they didn't allow no pregnant girls at school. I didn't do a lot of showing initially and I didn't tell no one at school about my condition. I didn't gain a lot of weight neither, so not many people knew it. I didn't know nothing about being pregnant. I was scared to drink water because I was scared I was going to drown the baby inside of me. How was I supposed to know the baby was in a bag? People just didn't talk about where babies come from or how they grew inside you. If you saw a pregnant woman walking down the street, that was unusual. Or if a woman your mama knowed got pregnant and you didn't see her for a while and if you asked where she was, your mama said things like, "Oh she broke her leg," for that's what women said about other pregnant women. If a woman got pregnant she disappeared.

Reuben and me got married on the front porch of Mama and

Daddy's apartment in Trenholm Court, June 30, 1963, on my six-teenth birthday. The sun was shining so pretty one minute, then the next it was thunder and lightning, then it was raining, then the rain was gone. Just before the service started I was getting ready still and Mama and Willela were helping me and my sister was looking at the clock saying, "We got to go," and then I started crying. Mama helped me dry my tears and Willela looked at the clock again and said, "We got to go," again, and I started crying again, and it went on like that for some time.

Eventually I made it to the altar. Or to the front porch as it was. Oh, I hoped—I hoped they wasn't just words that Reuben said to me: love and honor and cherish 'til death do us part. I hoped they wasn't just words I was saying back to him neither. One of my girl-friends from school was my maid of honor. She was crying. I won-dered what she was crying for. I was the one who should have been crying.

They held the reception over at Reuben's mama's house. My sis-ters and brothers were all there and some of our friends from school. We got wedding presents, towels and sheets and dishes. The plan was to live with Reuben at his parents' house, so that's where we spent the first night except I was crying so much it wasn't no honey-moon for neither of us. I didn't want to live at Reuben's mama's house. All night I stayed up looking out the window and crying. Fi-nally Reuben said, "All right, if you stop crying I'll take you back to Trenholm Court." That shut me up. So the next morning he walked me back to my mama's house and that's where I lived from then on, same as always. Reuben went back to the air base in Mississippi the next day.

Our baby was born November 19, 1963. About midnight the day before I felt like I had indigestion. Mama and Willela drove me to the hospital at Maxwell Air Force Base because my baby's daddy was in the military. Shawn was born about six in the morning. He was a beautiful boy, all scrunchy and fat, but I was scared of him and asked the nurse to take him out to the nursery. She did and brought him back later for me, but I told her I had a headache and needed some more sleep. She took the baby out and brought him back after a while and I had to think up another excuse then, but all I could think of was the headache again and this time she was onto me because she said I needed to keep the baby with me this time. I tried to give Shawn a bottle and he sounded like he was choking. I tried it again but he burbled and spit and I thought he was going to die for sure so that was enough of that. We went back to Trenholm Court after a day or two and I paid Mama to look after him for me. I was getting some money sent to me out of Reuben's military pay, so I gave Mama $25 a week for babysitting and another $50 for me and Shawn staying there.

My daddy never said nothing about it when I was pregnant at first, not so much as a by your leave, but he kept having this hurt look in his eyes whenever he looked at me, particularly since Reuben had asked him to date me in the first place and Daddy took such care to question him. I never knew if Daddy was hurting for me or was hurt by me. But when the baby was born, Daddy took to little Shawn like as if he was one of his own.

So with Shawn out of me, and me looking normal again, I decided to go back to high school. Shawn was a good baby, just happy with normal night wakings and things like that. My mama would hear the baby and fix a bottle and I'd go back to sleep. You weren't allowed to come back to high school if you'd had a baby so I told the principal I had been sick. That musta worked because they let me in but it was halfway through the year and I felt far behind and I didn't want to go back and repeat the grade so eventually I just quit high school altogether. It seemed like the thing to do, although I felt bad about not finishing more than the tenth grade.

Reuben came home every once in a while on leave and he wanted me to be with him when he came home. That made it tough to go to high school too. He was home for up to two weeks at a time and he wanted me staying over at his mama's house, being with him and all. I couldn't do no studying whenever Reuben came home and actually I hoped there'd be more of him being home, and so I figured high school was just getting in the way. I kept asking him if I could go to Mississippi where he was staying. I told him I'd bring Shawn with me and we could stay together as a family. He said Mississippi wasn't no good and we'd be together soon enough and to just be patient and so I waited. He was getting orders to go to London soon, he said, and when he went over there he'd save up enough money for me and Shawn to come over and be together as a family. So that's what kept me going. It was Reuben's decision. It was always somebody else making decisions for me. I was never asked what I wanted to do. I never had the opportunity to say.

Sometimes Reuben sent me letters from Mississippi asking me to send him some of the money the military was taking out of his pay for me, and I always did. I figured with me not going to high school no more and with Mama taking care of Shawn that I should get a job and so I did. I found work in a sewing factory and I was seventeen soon and they made me a supervisor right off because I guess I showed some capacity for that. I was made supervisor in the packing department and kept up with all the pressed pants and skirts and kept work flowing to each person doing the sewing but I never did sew. I wasn't good at it, really. I made $2.70 an hour for forty hours a week and it was 1964 and that was enough to buy diapers and baby food, and I took the bus back and forth to work.

Reuben moved to London all right with the service, so that left me even more time to myself. One day we heard that Stevie Wonder was coming to town. Stevie Wonder was just starting out but he was real cool already and he was going to play at the Ritz Theater in Montgomery and most people who went there knew it was full of rats. I had enough money for the show and took my brothers with me, Edward and Tom and Howard. Only blacks came to the show. Sure enough there was plenty of nibbling and scurrying and we hollered both for Stevie when he was on the stage and at the rats when the lights went down. That was what it was like to see a show in a theater for coloreds. Nothing much had changed in the last few years as far as that goes.

But the whole movement for change kept rolling along too. Daddy wasn't feeling too well those days but he kept us up on the news and he kept encouraging us to march with the MIA. It was all a little scary. We heard how the Freedom Riders were attacked in Alabama while testing compliance with bus desegregation laws, and how police attacked children with dogs and fire hoses at a march over in Birmingham, and how the Alabama governor stood in a schoolhouse door to stop university integration, and how Medgar Evers, who directed NAACP operations in Mississippi, was shot and killed by a sniper at his home after he had led a campaign for integration, and how on a sultry day in August a whole two hundred and fifty thousand Americans marched on our nation's capital in support of civil rights, and how in September of that same year, four schoolgirls, Addie Mae Collins, Denise McNair, Carole Robertson, and Cynthia Wesley, were getting ready for church services in Birmingham when a bomb exploded at the Sixteenth Street Baptist Church and killed them all, and how a segregationist rally was held in the aftermath of the Sixteenth Street bombings and a thirteen-year-old boy, Virgil Lamar Ware, was riding on the handlebars of his brother's bicycle when he was shot and killed by some white boys at that rally. It went on and on. Someplace there must be hope, folks must have known it, but hope seemed a mighty long ways off still. Every colored person I knowed was involved in some way in the movement. Every week Edward and my nephews walked to the MIA offices to see what was going on. I didn't know much what I could do, but I helped make sandwiches at the First Baptist Church for the Selma-to-Montgomery marches, and I marched myself whenever I could.

Parts of life felt good because of the movement, as strong and uncontrollable as it was, but other parts of life felt miserable in other ways. Like my stomach hurt most mornings. I didn't know if it was the stress of having a baby or working all the time or the marching or Reuben being gone or what. I was allowed to go to the doctor on base, so I went and they ran some tests. Turns out one of my kidneys was not tethered and was floating free and was clear around by my stomach. The doctor said I was one in a million to have a condition like that and there wasn't much they could do for it and if it didn't bother me much to just leave it be. "We'll just watch it," he said. So that's what we did.

Reuben sent me letters from London. He was telling me it wasn't gonna be much time 'til we was all gonna be together. But one day I received a letter that gave me a start. It was addressed to me all right, but the letter inside was from another girl writing to Reuben's mama. The other girl was stationed over in London, same as Reuben, and she mentioned how she couldn't wait to meet Reuben's family, and how she was so in love with their son. Oh, she went on and on about how fine Reuben was and how much fun they always had together and how she was so happy that they was so in love. I just sat down I was so stunned, but when I read it through some more times I thought about it and things made more sense. That other girl was no fool. She knew exactly what she was doing by putting the letter in the envelope addressed to me like that. She wanted me to know that she was in the picture and that she knew about me and that she was aiming to move me aside.

Turns out she already had. I wrote Reuben about it right away but he swore he didn't know anything about it. Reuben said it musta been somebody just trying to be smart. But later when I talked to Reuben's mama about it she looked at the floor and hugged me real tight and said she was so sorry, so sorry. She had knowed about that other girl in London and she was sorry her son could sometimes be that way, and to make matters worse the other girl was pregnant with Reuben's baby and things was real messed up.

It came as no surprise that shortly after that the little money I was getting every month from Reuben's paycheck stopped flowing. I wrote Reuben's commanding officer about it saying I was Reuben's wife and I had his baby at home and could use the money but he wrote back saying there was nothing he could do about things. The money from Reuben never started flowing again.

My husband came home to see Shawn soon after that. Shawn was just over two years old. Reuben brought him a toy truck. It was the last thing he ever bought him. That's when Reuben and I had the conversation. He brought it up actually but I knowed it was coming. He said we needed to do this for a time and we could get back together when things settled down, but I knowed they wouldn't be settling down. We left Shawn at Mama's house and we walked downtown to the lawyer's office and we walked out divorced. Reuben walked me home, and that was that. I wasn't mad at him. Not anymore. I knowed that he was that way and that was who he was gonna be. I wasn't mad at him at all. I just knowed we was never gonna be married in the way I had hoped we would be married. I knowed I couldn't make a marriage work neither. That's what I was feeling, at least. I never had a real chance to be a wife. I never knew what it was like to cook him a supper on a regular basis. Reuben had his faults and I knew those, but I also blamed myself. If only I had tried a little harder. Maybe there was something I could have done different. Reuben and me parted company as friends, which I was happy about, and we would be friends of some sorts or another from then on.

After that I had Shawn and my job, but that's all that was in my life. I had stopped going to church and I didn't feel connected to God. I guess when you do stuff and you know it's wrong, that's what happens. I had stopped going to church when I became pregnant. You didn't go to church if you was pregnant like I became pregnant. But I kept praying. I kept talking to God outside on the porch at night whenever I felt like he might be listening. But I wasn't reading no Bible then, nothing like that, and most nights when I prayed, God seemed a long way off.

Life became a cycle of work and coming home to the projects and work and coming home. I felt tired a lot. I knowed my life wasn't turning out right, not the way I hoped it should have. When I came home there was always a bottle to fix or a diaper to change or a spill to wipe or some laundry to do or a night when I heard crying and Mama said after a while that it would need to be me who got up and see what was the matter. Things was hard as a single parent, especially as a teenager. What did I know? How did I know how to be a parent or to take care of a baby? I still felt like a baby myself. I needed somebody to take care of me. Here I had made all these big decisions in my life—I had made them, but I didn't want to make them. Maybe I had allowed other people to make decisions for me and maybe I just went along with them, but the decisions were made one way or another, and I was living with the consequences now.

When I walked to the bus stop and at work I felt eyes on my back like there was a stigma to being a single mother and divorced. All the folks I had ever knowed got married and stayed married. It all seemed to come clear to me one particular day—it musta been about a month after my divorce and I had just come home from work. It was a Friday and I was feeling weary and I collected Shawn from my mama and carried him back to my bedroom where he had a crib—just us two alone. Everything was dark as I walked in, and when I turned on the fluorescent light it buzzed and made the room seem blue and colder than it really was. There was nothing cooking on the stove, for I had come home later and Mama was through in the kitchen. There was no sound from any other room. I fixed a bottle for Shawn and gave him some crackers and laid him down in his crib to sleep and sat on the sofa by myself trying to think of what my options were. I knowed this wasn't what I had hoped for, but I couldn't think of any way my life could become any better. I'd never go into the WAC or get any higher education or open my own restaurant like I had once dreamed.

My stomach was hurting again so I got up to see if there was something in the fridge easy to fix. I looked at myself in the mirror by the hall closet as I passed by. I took a good long look and this is who I saw: I saw a high school dropout living in the projects with no real work skills or hope for advancement other than the sewing factory. I saw a divorced single mom, teenaged and stupid and black. At least that's what I told myself I saw.

Who was gonna help me now?

6

Poor Choices

SYLVESTER WOULD HELP ME. THAT'S who. Although that thought was not in my mind's forefront, it was driving my actions as surely as the yellow-and-white bus was driving me down the street. The city bus I was riding in belched out smoke and dusted to a stop and a young man climbed aboard. He tossed his fare in the hopper and started making his way to the back where I sat.

By law in 1965 in Montgomery we could sit wherever we wanted to in a bus, but in practice it was still the whites near the front and the coloreds near the back. The man was taking his time and he ambled his way down the aisle toward me. The bus growled to life and the man grabbed the handrail to steady himself and for a moment he stood not moving.

He was slender and fine with his button-down shirt and skinny tie and pressed slacks. He looked like a real cool daddy, I thought, as he took out a handkerchief to wipe the sweat off his brow. I would never admit that he was fine. I would never admit that because I wasn't looking for no man. So why did I edge closer to the window to make it look like there was more room next to me? It's true I wasn't looking for nobody, but it's also true that there was nobody in my life just then—and those two truths have a mighty way of canceling each other out.

The man caught his balance as the bus shifted gears again. He took another step, returned his handkerchief to his pocket, and smiled all teeth. "Hey girl, this seat taken?" he said in my direction. I shook my head, and the man sat. I could have said that the seat was taken. I could have made up a story it was my husband who was getting on at the next stop, or my boyfriend, or my mama who I was meeting. I could have lied so the man would have never sat down. But I told the truth because I was alone, and the man sat, and that one decision would bump the shaky card in my life that was holding up the rest of the deck.

Oh it was a mighty warm day. Oh, yes, the weather had been mighty warm all week. I fanned myself with my bus pass and smiled, and for several miles the talk between us was more weather this and more weather that. Sylvester wasn't no military man, not enlisted or nothing, but he worked in the commissary on base in the meat department and it was a good job, he said. He rode the bus often, he told me, and I felt my face growing hot because I remembered that he had glanced in my direction previously on the bus, and I hoped I had looked away in time so as not to be seen staring at him. I was riding the bus quite a bit just then because my kidney was bothering me still and there was a doctor on base who I could see for not much cash money because I was still related to a military man, by child, even though my divorce from Reuben had come through.

"Oooooh, that's no joke," Sylvester said. "You poor girl. It's no fun to be seeing the doctor all the time." His eyes were soft and for the next mile the talk of warm weather changed to talking about my care. It was a pleasant way to talk to this man, and the next time Sylvester sat down beside me on the bus he remembered our talking from the week earlier, and he acted the same sweet way still. "Well what did the doctor say?" and "How you feeling?" and "That's a shame to be always seeing the doctor," he said this time, and there was more talk about the warm weather, although on this bus ride that sort of small talk was cut shorter and soon we was quiet together. Sylvester nudged his way closer to me as the bus rattled along, and I felt his thigh pressing through his pants against my dress. The brush must have been nothing, I told myself; surely there was no intention behind it. But I didn't move my thigh away, and sure enough there was still his leg pressed up against mine as we sat in the bus and the countryside rolled along. Sylvester was a cool daddy just like Reuben was a cool daddy, but the difference was that Reuben wasn't around no more and Sylvester was here. This new man was sitting right next to me, and this new man was talking right to me and he was remembering what I said. And this new man was still right here next to me a week later, and he was still saying nice things to me, and that constant stream of "right here" goes a powerful way to creating a kind of hopeful scream in a young girl's heart.

"So how your mama and daddy getting along, anyway?" he asked. Sylvester had met my mama and daddy before. His mama stayed in Trenholm Court, so he knew the area well. No, he didn't live there himself, he said when I asked outright. Sylvester stayed with his uncle in an apartment up close to the Booker T. school. It was different than when he lived in the court, Sylvester said. Whoops, that musta came out as a slip, because when I pressed him further on it he admitted he had stayed in Trenholm Court for several years while growing up although he hadn't told me that at first. We had ridden the bus several times together by then, and he had never told me he had ever stayed in Trenholm Court. I never would have let him sit next to me a second time if I had knowed that. Nothing good never came from Trenholm Court. But when he asked for my phone number I gave it to him anyway, and he gave me his, so I musta been feeling forgiving about his withholding the truth.

We stepped off the bus at the base and he went to his job at the meat market and I went my separate way to see the doctor. As I walked into the doctor's office I swore I wasn't looking for nobody, I really wasn't. Sylvester and I had just struck up a conversation, that was what I told myself as I waited while other people went ahead of me. And then we had struck up another, and then we was riding the bus all the time together, and that wasn't much of anything, I said to myself. The doctor measured my pulse and my blood pressure and both were racing, and the next week when I saw Sylvester again we had just struck up another conversation, I said to myself, then another and another, and sure enough just like that we was dating. Ain't nothing like a new dating relationship to make your feel good about yourself, I told myself as the doctor probed my abdomen, particularly when you've just lost a husband and your soul has this gash in it as tall as the man who left you. As I stood in line to pay my bill and smelled the clean antiseptic smell of the doctor's office, I told myself that all was new now, and I was just cleaning up my life from the hurt that the last boyfriend had brought into my life, and Sylvester just made me feel so good about things, he rightly did. When I rode the bus home from the doctor I had the biggest smile on my face, like all was gonna be right with the world. I knew it rightly so.

There wasn't no talk about getting serious. We wasn't in love, nothing like that. We went to the movies and he paid. He bought me popcorn and it was warm, fresh popcorn with a heap of melted country butter just the way I liked it, and our hands brushed against each other in the popcorn tub when we both went in for kernels at the same time. He even opened the door for me as he was taking me home from the movies, and I had to admit that I loved holding the arm of a man. Mama had said once to me that it's easy to get attracted to all sorts of bad things when they seem all innocent at first.

That voice went around in my head as I was walking out of the theater holding the arm of this man, but I must admit I wasn't listening much to Mama's voice just then.

Soon Sylvester and me was seeing each other three times a week. He was so friendly. So kind. So nice and sweet. He kissed me and I let him. He put his hands on me and I let him. Then we was in his room together on his bed and I wasn't saying no. You think you're playing hard to get and being all cool, but there was Sylvester's kisses and his hands and his bed and his sweet nothings being whispered in my ear and so I gave in. It wasn't easy for me this time neither. It felt like a sin to me still, and when we was putting on our clothes I swore I wouldn't let it happen again. But the next night it did. And two times the next week after that. Mama's voice was still rolling around my head saying it's easy to allow yourself to get talked into doing things you don't want to do, particularly when you're not in the habit of making decisions for yourself. But I wasn't listening.

Sure enough, a month went by and nothing was there when it should have been. Then another month went by and I felt so crazy and foolish again. How did this happen? I didn't know nothing about birth control. You didn't talk about those things with nobody. You just didn't. Five days after I should have got my period the second month I sat in my room staring out the window. Outside was gray and I gazed at the red dirt yard and the lines of laundry blowing in the wind, and the road next to the apartment was dirty. I had to tell mama, but what was I gonna say? Hi Mama, this is so funny—you'll never guess what happened again. Hi Mama, people will be saying, oooh you look so young to be a grandma again. Hi Mama, guess what: my life is a mess.

"Hi Mama," I said. My voice choked. Mama was fixing a pot of peas on the stove. I swallowed and tightened my stomach to get the nerve. "I gots something I needs to tell you."

She paused and wiped her hands on her apron. I couldn't say no more. She saw my tears and she didn't make no fuss. She just came over and hugged me. "Oh well, Martha," she said. "Oh well. You made your bed. Now you're gonna have to lie in it." She didn't say it to be mean-like. She said it as fact. What could she say?

I never told Daddy outright about my second pregnancy. Mama told him for me. If you can't talk to your mama about these things, how you ever gonna talk to your daddy? Daddy never said nothing to me about it, neither good nor bad. He got up the next morning and went to his job at the fertilizer factory, and I got up and went to my job at the sewing factory, and Mama kept cooking and ironing and tending baby Shawn, and that's how things went.

Of course I needed to tell Sylvester. I thought about going over to his apartment later the next evening after I told Mama, but he would start to kiss me hello and then I would need to put my hand to his chest and hold him back and I didn't want to be touching him just then, so I phoned. My voice was shaky but I managed to get out what needed to be said.

"What?" he said. "How did this happen?"

"How do you think it happened?"

"Are you sure?"

"Yeah I'm sure."

"What you gonna do about it?"

"I don't rightly know, Sylvester. I don't rightly know."

He said he'd see me later and he hung up. It felt so dark in the living room. I started to cry and walked to my bedroom so nobody would see me. Shawn was sleeping in his crib. I looked at him, his sweet dark face, his eyes shut tight against the world. Two babies. That's what I'd soon have in my family. Two babies and me.

I kept working at the factory right up until it was time to give birth. Not much was showing for quite a while so it wasn't hard to not tell nobody. Besides, I needed the money. Sylvester wasn't helping none. There was no talk of marriage and no talk of him helping out. None at all. I wasn't seeing much of him anyway. I went to work and came home and ate supper and sat in my room. Most nights I cried. I found I didn't know how to turn off the tears. I tried to stop crying. I really did. But I couldn't. I just couldn't. I didn't know what was wrong with me. I just couldn't stop crying.

When it came time, I went to the hospital on base again. The doctor checked me in the delivery room; my feet were up in the stirrups. "You've got two heartbeats in there," he announced. "You're going to have twins."

"No, no no," I said, my voice rising to a shout. "I'm too little. I can't have twins." The pushing and grunting began but only one baby came out. The doctor must have heard some other heartbeat inside me because there wasn't no two babies within me. There was no explanation given for the wrong diagnosis and certainly no apology for making me fret so. I just felt happy there was only one baby. My son Quintin was born February 25, 1966, about 11 at night. He was healthy, seven pounds, six ounces, and sucked his milk no problem. I wasn't as scared about a new baby this time like I was when Shawn had been born. I had some idea of what to do. We went home in a day or so, just like last time, and Mama helped out right away and I was able to go back to work soon. Sylvester came around and visited Quintin within a week. Sylvester came and left and went back to his apartment and that's all he did. There was never any money provided for Quintin's care. I so longed for Sylvester to be the kind of husband and father I dreamed somebody would be in my life. No one wants to be having kids and being by yourself. But as much as I hoped he would do the right thing, nothing much changed. How stupid I was. How completely crazy I was to ever hope like that about a man.

About this time I gathered the little cash money I had and moved out on my own. I figured that maybe if I had my own place then Sylvester would be coming around more. Maybe he would want to be with me and his baby and Shawn. I moved down the street to another apartment at Trenholm Court. The sewing factory gave me a raise to $3.30 an hour and I was able to pay rent in the projects with that. Mama kept my kids during the day. I liked my new apartment because I could cook on my own and sometimes I pretended I was working in my own restaurant. I fixed supper for Shawn and Quintin and pretended they was my customers and that they was feeling good in my restaurant eating all the good food I made. For myself I fixed grits in the morning, a sandwich for lunch, and for dinner I'd make corn bread, gravy, and Salisbury steak when I had the money for it. My stomach kept hurting more and more, so sometimes I made chicken and dumplings and found that I was only eating the soft dumplings because that's all I felt like eating.

One day I was washing dishes when I noticed a girl stopping in front of my apartment. She was about my age, maybe a year or two younger, nothing particularly pretty to look at. I guessed she was about the same as me. She didn't look angry or nothing. Mostly she looked earnest. When she came up and knocked on my door she made it real clear that she had something important she wanted to say to me.

"Is Sylvester here?"

"No," I said. "Why you want to know?"

"I just want to know where he is."

"Well, he ain't here. I don't know where he is."

She paused for a moment, then looked straight at me. "You should know that me and Sylvester go together." She said it matter-of-factly. Then she stood there saying nothing.

I paused and looked at her. "Okay," I said. That's all I said. What was I going to say? How would you feel if someone came to your house telling you this? I felt foolish. We stood there a moment, this girl and me, just looking at each other sizing each other up. Then I shut the door. The experience reminded me of what I went through with Reuben. I walked to the kitchen and phoned Sylvester.

"It ain't no thing," he said. "She's just a friend. She ain't nothing more."

A few days later I was downtown walking past Newberry's Five-and-Dime, and over on the other side of the street I saw that same girl and Sylvester walking together, talking and laughing. My babies were back home at Mama's house and I was shopping alone. For a moment I thought about running over there and making a scene, but what would that have done? If a person is with a person, then that's who they want to be with. Why look foolish? So I didn't say nothing. An hour later I was at home and Sylvester came by my apartment. "Hey Martha," he said. "I saw you downtown. Why didn't you come over and talk?"

"Because you was with someone," I said.

"Yeah, but that was okay. She wouldn't have minded."

"Well I minded."

"So what you saying?"

"I'm saying you can't be with her and me both. You got to choose which girl you want to be with and then be with that girl."

"Why do I got to do that?" he asked.

I turned back toward the apartment and was quiet for a moment. "So that's your answer?" I said. Turning toward him again I studied his face, hoping I'd see a flicker of more. Sylvester stuck his hands in his pockets and didn't say nothing. He just stood there quiet. He always had something to say, but he was so quiet just then. "I gotta go," I said and closed the door.

The relationship was over then. We both knew it. There was never much of a relationship to begin with. It didn't hurt much this time to think that it was over. From that day forward we never kissed or nothing again. We was completely through. But results have an uncanny way of carrying over from actions you did in your past. The month after we broke up I missed my period again. Then came the second month and there was still nothing. Man oh man I felt crazy, like a broken record spinning round and round. I looked in my bathroom mirror and scowled. "Stupid!" I shouted to my reflection and shook my head. "Stupid! Stupid! Stupid!"

Sylvester kept calling and trying to talk with me, but I knew it was over, even though I was pregnant again with his second baby. If the trust is broken, it would be broken again, and it didn't make no sense to try to have a relationship with him. When there's no trust you don't have nothing. Finally I told him the news.

"Well what we gonna do?" he said.

"We ain't gonna do anything," I said. "It's my trouble. I'll deal with it." So that was that.

Telling Mama was harder this time. For a while I didn't say nothing. Finally one day we was sitting in the kitchen and she spoke up: "Martha, I think you're pregnant."

I lowered my head. "Yes ma'am. I think I am too."

She didn't say nothing for a while then. We both got up and moved to the living room where we sat. We wasn't watching no TV or listening to the radio. We was just sitting. Finally she sighed and said, "Where did my baby go wrong?" She wasn't looking at me. She was looking at the ceiling.

I was able to work at the sewing factory until I was eight months along, then I had to stop working. Reginald was born 8 o'clock in the morning, September 12, 1967. He was born at St. Jude's Hospital because I had a different doctor then. There was no complications, thank God. The baby was a good size with deep dark eyes and a chubby chin. I lay in my hospital bed for some time after they took Reginald to the nursery, just thinking. So now I got three kids to feed. I got no child support from neither man. This is what I'm gonna do then. I'm gonna take care of my boys.

Straightaway I went back to work. Mama looked after my sons and sometimes Reuben's mama did. She knew Reuben and me wasn't together because of him, and I guess that was one of the ways she figured she could help out. Reuben's mama took all three boys, even though only one of them was Reuben's. I was ever grateful she did that.

Nothing was different in my mind, though. I was still crying a lot. Every night now it seemed. Everything was always gonna be the same stupid thing in my life, no matter how hard I tried—that's what I figured. Everywhere I looked things was painful. That was how the whole world seemed just then. Everything was pain. Just pain and gashes and blood and darkness. That was how the movement was progressing anyway. We saw it every night on TV, and the pain of the movement seemed to mirror the pain in my life.

Daddy kept us up on the news when I couldn't see it for working late. He worked during the day in the heat and the dust and the
stink of the fertilizer factory, and when it was hot in the Alabama
summers he was on his feet standing up all day and it was hot for
him. At night he caught charley horses in his legs, real bad cramp-
ing, and he moaned and I brought ice to him when I was over at
their house. I knowed it was hard standing on your feet all day because that's what I did in the sewing factory, but I wasn't an old man
like Daddy. He was happy to retire from the fertilizer factory when
he turned sixty-five in the mid-sixties. Then he started worked as a
custodian at the elementary school and he started to forget things
too, but we never said anything to him because that might have hurt
his pride. And that's where he was working for the latter part of the
sixties when we kept hearing all the news on TV.

Right in our state of Alabama there was Samuel Younge Jr., shot
dead a few cities away in Tuskegee by a white gas station owner
after they argued about segregated restrooms. And Vernon Ferdi-
nand Dahmer, a businessman with lots of cash money, who offered
to pay the poll taxes for the coloreds who couldn't afford the fee required to vote. His house was firebombed and he died of his burns.
There was Wharlest Jackson who was promoted to a job that whites
normally had, so they put a bomb to his car and he died. And Ben-
jamin Brown, a civil rights organizer, who was watching a student
protest from the sidelines. He was hit with a stray gunshot from
police who had fired into the crowd. There was also Samuel Ham-
mond Jr., Delano Middleton, Henry Smith, all shot dead, shot dead,
shot dead. The names ran together after time like so much blood.

Then came April 4, 1968. I was sitting in the kitchen at Mama's
house and a cry came from the living room where the news was on
TV. It was Daddy's cry. He was standing up although his legs was
hurting, and he was pointing at the TV. Daddy's mouth was open,
his eyebrows tight and pained against his eyes. The news said he
had been shot dead on the balcony of a motel in Memphis. He

was dead. Martin Luther King Jr. was truly dead. At first the news seemed too painful to bear. Mama came into the living room and clasped her hands tight together and started to cry and some of my brothers and sisters were there and everybody started crying. For about an hour we just sat crying, staring out the window or looking at the floor. We had heard this man give so many great speeches and with him shot dead we wouldn't have no more speeches. He was our leader, the one making the sacrifices and putting himself on the line. Now our leader was shot dead. So we just sat and cried and didn't say nothing. After a few hours of sitting with no words we started wondering aloud what we was gonna do. Nobody had any good answers to that.

I certainly didn't have no good answers. Reverend King had a dream, like I once had a dream, and the news of his death went right through my heart. Somehow his dream and mine was all tangled up together. Everything was dead now. When I stopped going with Sylvester I swore off all relationships with all men, and I went kind of numb inside. I wasn't going to go with nobody and I wasn't looking neither. I swore it to myself. But along came this guy, James, who stayed just down the road from me in Trenholm Court. He was a nice-looking fella and twenty-six. I was twenty-three. It seemed I was always trying to shoo him off. He and I saw each other around at the store or at baseball games in the park. We talked and said hey, but it was never no big deal.

Then he asked me to go out to eat one time and like a fool I said yes. They had a restaurant downtown called the Stop In Chick In, and we ate there, then when we left he said he had a special surprise for me that evening. From out of his pocket he pulled a room key. That wasn't something I hadn't bargained for, but I guessed that he had bought me supper so I should be nice, and anyway I couldn't figure out a way to say no. I went to the hotel room with him. You could see some of the city from those windows, not many lights, but enough so it glowed pretty. We didn't see much of those lights nohow, because as soon as we got in the room he closed the blinds and turned the lights low. I didn't really want him to do that 'cause I had a pretty good idea what was coming, and sure enough he started kissing me and I let him because even though I was kinda numb inside I was also hurting and lonely, and his hands were all over me now, and I went along with it. When it was over I told myself I was so stupid again and I should have knowed what was gonna happen and that's the price you pay for not having the nerve to say no.

James asked me out again, but this time I did manage to say no. I didn't want to go to another hotel with him. There was nothing in his face or expression that sparked any sort of hope in me. I truly didn't want to be in a relationship with nobody. I wasn't playing hard to get. I just didn't think I knew how to make a relationship work. Any relationship. If you're looking back on your life and you're seeing how you messed up with all those other folks, then there's never a reason to think it's gonna be different with this one. So I told myself there was no use trying to make things work.

James and I were together only that one time there in the hotel room. Apparently that's all it took because sure enough I was pregnant again. In nine months I went to the hospital and the doctor had gone out somewhere and the nurses were all outside my door laughing and talking. They said the baby wasn't gonna come no time soon. There was another woman in the room with me and she was moaning and groaning and they kept checking on her but I wasn't making no noise so they figured I was all right. But I knew it was time and I tried to get the nurses' attention but they wasn't coming so I called louder and still nothing and so I picked up the lamp next to my bed and slammed it down as hard as I could. That got them running real quick. They rushed over a gurney and ripped my arm all bloody trying to get me on. As they was racing me down to the delivery room I huffed a time or two and the baby slipped out right there on the gurney. They had to track down a doctor to come cut the cord.

My fourth child—I was so sure it was gonna be a girl this time. I had her name picked out and everything: Velecia Renee. But my fourth child was born October 17, 1969, and he was a boy all right. My brother Tom picked a name for him because I didn't have no boys' names picked out. Tom named the baby Nyrone. Tom had just come back from the military and he knowed a fella there named Nyrone who was a pretty good guy. So that was my boy's name.

James came by a few days later. I was sitting on my mama's porch at her apartment.

"Why didn't you tell me you was having my baby?" he asked. "You could have told me."

"Would it have made a difference?" I asked.

"A difference?" He stepped forward, his fists clenched, and I thought he was gonna take a swing at me. "You are mean, Martha," he said. "You are a hateful woman. You could have at least told me what was going on."

I didn't say nothing to him. I let my gaze fall to the red dirt of the yard. James might have been saying other things at me just then, but I wasn't listening. I didn't want James to be a part of my life. I wouldn't have been no good for him neither. If he wanted to he could send money to take care of Nyrone, but that was all I wanted from him.

My four sons had three different daddies and none of them was around now. I needed help, that was true. As sure as Reverend King was dead, I needed a new dream. But there wasn't no man who was gonna help me now. Not Reuben or Sylvester or James. Mama and Daddy was there but they was just making their way, and I didn't want to be taking help from them no more now that I was supposed to be growed up. My brothers and sisters were all living lives of their own now—they wasn't gonna help me. God was far away—I knowed I was a sinner for sure. God wasn't in the business of helping out sinners like me.

There was only one thing I could do. I knowed it one day while working at the sewing factory. It was Friday, closing time, and I collected my check for $132 for that week's pay. That was the gross wage and I was gonna feed a family of five on that after the government started subtracting its cut from there. Ain't no government gonna help me, I knowed that for sure. While looking at that check I started walking for the door and I knowed there was only one person I could depend on. She was stupid and ugly but she was the only hope I had. If that's the way it was, then I would give it one final push. I would roll my sleeves to the elbow and press forward with everything I could give.

I stopped by the back door of the sewing factory. My stomach was hurting something fierce and the pain made me double over, but my bus was coming and I needed to hurry. Standing straight, I pushed open the door and went into the night.

7

Determined

ALL THAT WEEKEND I SCOURED the job ads in the newspaper, but nothing came up that was gonna pay me more than I was making at the sewing factory, and I knowed there was no future there. Late on Sunday night my sister-in-law phoned with a gleam of hope in her voice. A glass company in town was hiring. It was money, she said, big money—folks with college degrees was actually quitting their teaching jobs so they could work there. It sounded too good to be true.

Come Monday I ducked out of work at the sewing factory and went down to Brockway Glass to talk to the man about a new job. It was January 1970. A wind was blowing cold across the gravel parking lot and snow was rumored to be coming soon. Brockway was near the railway tracks on the other side of Montgomery. The compound was made up of a bundle of big corrugated sheds, and the whole factory looked like a bunch of airplane hangars plopped down in rows.

"You ain't finished high school," the man said as he glanced at my application. He ground a cigarette into the ashtray on his desk, squinted, and looked me up and down. It was cold in his office and I pulled my jacket tighter around my shoulders.

"No sir," I said. "But I'm a good worker and I can do the job."

"It's shift work," he said, blowing the last cigarette smoke out of his nose. "You got family?"

"Yes sir. Four boys. They young. That's why I need this job."

"Shift work ain't easy with family." He barked out the words. "You strong?"

"Yes sir. I can work day or night. Whatever hours you got for me."

"Metal sheds get hot in summer. Mighty cold in winter too. I don't want no complaining from my workers, you hear?"

"Yes sir. You won't hear no complaining from me."

He scratched his head and looked me over again. "Well I dunno," he said. "I just dunno."

As I shut the doors of the glass factory behind me, I shut out the noise of the assembly lines and the hollering of workers inside. The gravel scrunched under my feet as I hurried across the parking lot to get to the bus station down the road. My smile broke into a grin and my grin broke into a chuckle. I couldn't contain it any longer. I let loose with a long wild *Wahoo!* In my hand was a paper that was gonna settle my destiny. I had arrived, yes sir—Martha Hawkins had arrived at all things good. The job at Brockway paid $12 per hour, paid by check. It musta been near the highest-paying factory job in Montgomery. I didn't even know what I'd do with $12 per hour. We was millionaires!

Shift work came in three sets round the clock. For five days you worked one shift, then it changed to another shift for the next week, and so on. The first shift was graveyard, from midnight to 8 A.M.

Graveyard was no problem for me because my boys was all asleep then and I could call my nieces, Pam and Cassandra (we called her San), to come spend the night. The next shift was day, 8 A.M. to 4 P.M. That was my favorite because it felt like a regular job. The last shift was 4 P.M. to midnight, and that was the hardest for me. My boys were home from school and awake for much of that time, so when I worked that shift it meant I didn't see my boys all week long. When they was at school I was sleeping, and when they was at home I was at work.

The boys soon came to hate that middle shift as much as I did. "Mama, please don't go to work tonight," Quintin said late one afternoon after I had worked at Brockway about three months. "Please, please, please. Don't go. We don't get to see you when you're at work."

Shawn held Quintin by the shoulders and hauled him back a step. "Mama's got to go to work, fool," he said. He sounded so grown up for a seven-year-old. "You have a good night at work, Mama. You don't worry about us none."

I kissed them. I kissed them all. My boys. I hoped I didn't let them see how sorry I was feeling. I saved my tears until I got on the bus. It rips your heart to hear your boys saying those things—to not want you to go to work, to be so brave that they knew you had to go to work. Tears or no tears, we was moving on up, yes sir. The young Martha Hawkins family was moving on up.

I began at the bottom making boxes at Brockway, but in only six months I became a packer. It wasn't much more money, but it was more action. Box makers worked upstairs where there was nothing going on all day, while packers worked down on the floor with the belt lines. Twenty belts buzzed along day and night, with each belt making a different kind of glassware. The company fashioned a variety of different jars for jams or ketchup or pickles, whatever the other companies that contracted with Brockway needed. Being a packer meant I stood alongside a belt with another packer and we looked to see that nothing was wrong with the stream of glassware in front of us. If something wasn't good, you snatched it off the line and threw it in the discard pile, where it went back to the hot end to be remade. It wasn't hard work. You just had to be on your toes for eight hours and stand there watching stuff motor by. Shift after shift that's what I did.

First on my list: buying a car. I was gonna learn how to drive. No more taking the bus for Martha Hawkins, no sir. My first car was a brown Ford Pinto, one of those little hatchbacks that came with whitewall tires and not much more. The license plate slogan read, THE HEART OF DIXIE, like it was with all cars in Alabama then, but that amount of advertising for the Confederacy and all it had ever stood for surely didn't detract me from learning how to drive. You got to be practical about some of these things. My Pinto was a stick shift and I had no idea how to operate a manual transmission. I climbed in, started up my Pinto, and jolted down the street until I figured out how to let out the clutch while stepping on the gas evenly. In about a week I was a smooth operator. The boys drove with me to the grocery store and we all wore grins as big as hubcaps.

Next stop: a new place to live. That would happen about a year after landing the job at Brockway. Work at Brockway provided so much cash money that I could save up for a real down payment for a house. We was moving out of the projects for good. Some folks looked at you funny if you was colored and trying to buy a home in their neighborhood, but a new subdivision called Sheridan Heights had been built a year or two before and it was welcoming all kinds.

The house I bought for my boys to grow up in cost $30,000. Paying the mortgage would be steeper than I was used to, but I could meet the payments if I watched every dollar. When the sign on the front lawn said SOLD, I never felt prouder. I, Martha Hawkins, high school dropout, was a homeowner. Shawn grinned as he looked at that sign and gave Quintin a playful punch in the arm. Reginald raced across the yard. Nyrone toddled after him. I had bought a house. A real house.

Our new house sat on Faro Drive. Each house in the Sheridan

Heights subdivision looked similar to the one next to it. They was all made out of bricks with regular pitched roofs and a real grass lawn out front. This was a place for respectable folks, and it seemed everybody we knowed was moving to Sheridan or the neighboring subdivision called Brookview. I think every family in our neighborhood was first-generation homeowners. We was all learning how to become middle class.

Mama and Daddy had already moved in a few streets over. Daddy had been saving his money for years. Mama was so proud the day they moved out of the projects. Daddy always looked after her real good and she knew that. My sister Willela and her husband stayed right around the corner. Georgia and Alice and Rosa and their families stayed close by, and Edward and his family stayed just down the street from Mama and Daddy. Most of the greater Hawkins family was living within two miles of each other in this new place of opportunity. We all knew that the projects wasn't a good place to stay no more. Not sure if the projects ever had been good in the first place, but they certainly hadn't been good for years. There had always been gangs in the projects—chain gangs they called them because they fought other gangs with chains after football games—but now the gangs were getting rougher. Drugs was moving in and everything was becoming violent. You heard sirens coming and going most every night. Seems it was a whole new breed of folks moving in to the projects.

Our new house on Faro Drive had real carpet on the floor. It wasn't fancy but it was fine. The house came with three bedrooms—Nyrone and Shawn stayed in one, Reginald and Quint bunked in the other—and a real backyard for the kids to play in. There was even a den that I fixed up just how I liked it with a sofa and chair and a lamp. That was my quiet place, the place I could sit for a moment or two after work and collect my thoughts about how we was gonna keep on keeping on. That resolve was what kept driving me forward. This girl might have been ugly and stupid and already made her share of mistakes in her young life, but this girl was gonna set it right by sheer grit. There was only one person who was gonna help me, and that was me. It was by my might and power, and I was gonna get it done.

Sure, my daddy helped out plenty. Sheridan Heights might have been the new middle class, but it wasn't all safe, that's for sure. By 1970, schools had finally become integrated in Montgomery. A year or two after that was when my boys started going to school, and things was still unsettled. It wasn't uncommon for a colored boy to be walking down the street and hear a bunch of fellas yelling at him, "Nigger, go home!" or "You better run, boy! You better run!" School buses only picked up kids who lived five miles or more away, so my boys walked everywhere they needed to go as their school was just two miles away. Daddy took the boys to their ball games when I couldn't be there. Anytime Daddy walked the boys anywhere—to school, to the bus, to their games, if they was still young enough to not be embarrassed by it—Daddy held their hands. To see this big grandpa walking straight and tall next to these young boys drew a clutch at my heart. Daddy was all the father they'd ever need. Ain't gonna be nobody messing with his grandchildren as long as he was around.

About that time is when I decided I was gonna be the best mama I could be to my boys. If they needed strength and love and discipline, then I was gonna be all that to them and more. On Friday nights we had a Bible study, just me and the boys in our den. I wasn't reading the Bible much, but I knowed the boys needed all the goodness shoveled inside them that they could get, so I made each boy read a chapter out of Psalms or Proverbs and then explain to the other boys what it meant as best he could. The boys who were listening were required to ask questions of the boy doing the explaining. I gave away prizes, 50¢ or even $1 when I had a spare one, for whoever asked the most questions. The boys and me did the Bible study every week. If not on Friday, then on Monday. The boys was okay with the plan. If they sassed me about it I didn't hesitate setting them straight. That's how I was raised and it didn't do me no harm.

I knowed the boys needed to have a strong work ethic, so I set them to doing chores. They had lists. One boy was to wash dishes. Another was to sweep floors. Bathrooms needed cleaning and carpets needed vacuuming. If a boy was too young to reach the dishes, then he could pull a chair over to the sink. Reginald thought it was fun doing dishes because he got to splash around in soapy water. But Quint told him he was doing girl's work and then Reginald thought doing dishes wasn't fun no more, but I knowed that doing dishes didn't hurt the boys none. Come Saturday morning there was no such thing as sleeping in. At 7 A.M. the boys was up, cleaning themselves and getting shined, making their beds, getting ready for the day. There was lawn to be cut in warm months, and they could work in the garden at my mama's house. I wasn't gonna raise no lazy boys. I had seen too many lazy boys become lazy men, and I wanted none of that for my sons.

The boys went to Chisholm Elementary School and later to Goodman Junior High. A few years earlier Chisholm had been an all-white school and it was rumored to still be a stronghold of the Klan. I know Daddy had talks with my boys about that. "You never go picking fights for yourself," he told them. "But if someone comes after you, then you be sure to defend yourself, you hear?" One day Daddy was walking Shawn home from school and a rookie policeman pulled his cruiser over next to them and started asking a lot of questions. Shawn told me the story when he got home. The young policeman was calling my Daddy "boy," though Daddy was in his sixties, and Daddy was burning up about how the policeman talked to him—and it took an awful lot for Daddy to get hot about anything. But Daddy kept answering the man's questions courteously, Shawn said, and then just kept telling Shawn to "keep walking, just keep walking." Daddy had a lot of talks with the boys about that kind of thing. He made sure that if he wasn't around to walk with them that they walked together in a group for protection. One day he took Shawn aside and told him that as the oldest he was to be the leader and needed to set the tone for the rest of the boys in the house and at school. Daddy whupped my boys occasionally, and that was fine by me, but I don't think he never needed to whup Shawn. Shawn was by the book from the get-go. "All a man has is his word," Daddy told Shawn. "So you make sure you always look a man in his eye and talk straight to him with deepness in your voice. Keep your back up when you walk, and if you tell someone you're gonna do something, then you do it."

When it came to school, I had other concerns for my boys. Each year on the first day I took my boys to school and had a talk with each boy's teacher. I always gave the teachers the same speech: "I'm a single parent working swing shifts at the factory, so I ain't got no time to be coming down to the school if my boy ever gets in trouble. If that happens—and I know it will—then I give you full permission to light him up." Some of the teachers looked surprised when I said that, but I never had a teacher turn me down on that offer. Whuppings was okay by me if the teacher did it right and the boy needed it. Reginald got the most. He needed those whuppings, that's for sure.

For a real treat I took the boys to McDonald's. That was when I was most proud of them. Maybe Shawn did well in baseball, or Quint brought home A's. When they done me proud I'd say, "Boys, we're going to McDonald's," and Nyrone's eyes would light up. "Mama, going to McDonald's is just like going to Disney World," Reginald said to me once before chomping into a Big Mac.

I likened my job as parent to a coach. The boys were the athletes. I ran the team. If one of the boys fought with his brother, I made them make up and hug. There was no way they was gonna grow up not loving their brothers. Reginald was the joker and he could always mix it up with anybody. Shawn was straight and narrow. Quint was laid back. Nyrone was the mix of them all.

"Boys," I said at Bible study one Friday night. "Family is the most important thing you'll ever have. You will have friends in life, fellas who'll be just like your brothers, but you'll never have anything as important as your real brothers. When you get into it, that's all you got." The boys nodded in seriousness and I could tell something was sinking in. That night I fixed them roast turkey with real gravy and dressing. The boys smacked their lips and asked for seconds on the dressing and gravy. Like everything else I cooked, I cooked a whole lot of love into that gravy. The boys told me they knowed that someday that gravy would become famous.

But I wasn't eating much myself that particular Friday night. After I cooked for the boys, I went into my bedroom by myself, shut the door, and lay on the bed holding my stomach. I wasn't feeling right again. I hadn't been saying much about that to the boys, but it had gone on for some time now. When the lights were all out at night is when I did my crying.

That night the pain was becoming something fierce. Maybe if I just lay down long enough it would go away. An hour went by but my stomach was hurting even more now. It hurt like someone had taken the insides and peeled them back to show the outsides. As good as everything was looking on the outside of my life right now, everything inside me was raw. As the hours went by the pain was getting worse. It was late but I wondered if I should phone Mama. Maybe she would know what to do.

On the way to the phone I had to stop by the bathroom. There it was again. I had been feeling this dull nausea every day for some time now, but every once in a while I got this real sharp jab like someone was sticking a hot knife into my right side. I heaved everything inside of me into the toilet. I had been doing a lot of that lately too. Wasn't nothing much in my stomach as I hadn't been eating for a spell, and the waves kept coming as I shuddered with the dry heaves. I decided to go back to bed and see if it would pass.

Mama took me to the doctor on Monday afternoon. I clocked out of work to go. Daddy took the boys to the ballpark after school. The doctor took X-rays then came into the examination area. His eyebrows were raised. "It's a good thing you came in when you did," he said. "You need to get to a hospital right away."

"But I got to get back to work," I said. "I ain't got time to go to the hospital."

"Well, you better," the doctor said. "It's your appendix. It's burst."

They rushed me to the hospital and cut me open that same evening for emergency surgery. My mama was by my bed the next morning. My head felt woozy, like a stream of snake's venom was still running through my veins. Mama's cool hand stroked my forehead. I could feel the scar where the appendix had come out. I hadn't realized the full extent of my sickness before but I was feeling it right now after surgery, that's for sure. "Mama," I said. "Your baby's sick. She's real sick."

"Shhhhh Martha," Mama said. "You just lie still. Your daddy's got the boys. Everything's fine. You just sleep now. Just sleep."

I missed six weeks' work because of my burst appendix. Disability insurance kept the bills at bay. Disability didn't pay as much as a regular paycheck, but it got us by 'til I was on my feet again. If you get bucked off a horse, you got up and got back on, that's what I figured, anyway.

A bit of time passed before the next blow came my way. I was back at work for night shift one week and feeling crampy. I excused myself off the line and went to the employees' bathroom and doubled over in the stall from the pain. Blood was all over in the water when I stood up. I never knew I had that much blood in me.

I went to the doctor the next day and he gave me some pills and said things might clear up so I waited some time, but every day it seemed more blood came out of me. The cramps kept me laid up in bed when I come home after work. I took pills by the handful, but no matter how many I took there was always another cramp coming. A month went by and then another and then a few more and some days I was okay but most days I had real heavy bleeding. After a while of this they put me in the hospital again, and this time they gave me a hysterectomy. I wasn't yet twenty-six. They took out my uterus through the same scar as my appendix. I missed more work but the disability kept the bills paid again.

Some more time passed and I thought I was clear of feeling bad, but then a third hurdle came my way. Again I was at work and my forehead was feeling hot this time. But I couldn't miss work again—they was starting to say I was being sick all the time, and they was right about that. So I tightened myself up and kept going. I didn't tell no one I was feeling miserable. Who would I tell?

A week passed and then another and I was having a fever most days but I just kept on keeping on. Then a month passed and another month and it's amazing how you can keep going when you put your mind to it. At home one day from swing shift I stood at the top of my stairs getting ready to step down and everything around me was suddenly colored different, just swirly, and then all was dark. "Mama, wake up! Mama, wake up!" Shawn kept saying to me over and over again. He was kneeling next to me at the bottom of the stairs when I came to. I had tumbled down the whole flight. Shawn ran and got his grandmother and they took me to the hospital where they took my temperature: 105 degrees.

The doctor said it was a kidney stone and it would pass soon, so he put me in the hospital where they started a steady input of cranberry juice and aspirins. Some days went by and I kept sweating out of my hospital clothes. Nurses changed me but my fever kept the sweat coming, and I was lying in pools of water by the hour. Seemed like the doctor was always missing my room and no kidney stone had passed yet, so I wanted to hear it for myself. I wrestled myself to my feet, made sure my gown wasn't flopping at the back, and stood in the doorway where I knowed the doctor must be passing by soon. Sure enough, he came down the hall and I hollered for him that something must be wrong. If I was just waiting for this thing to pass, I had boys to look after at home and I could wait there same as I could wait in the hospital. He said fine, go home, but make sure you keep drinking that cranberry juice. So I walked out of the hospital. Something didn't sound right to me about what the doctor said, so I had the sense to find a phone book and call a kidney specialist. The specialist made me an appointment for the next day, and when he saw my test results his eyebrows were raised too, just like that first doctor's, and he said it wasn't no kidney stone but a kidney infection, and everything in that area in me looked all busted up inside. He gave me some different medicine and said I needed to go back to the hospital, but I wanted to see my boys so I went home. That evening I had the worst headache in a long while and started throwing up something fierce, so I called the doctor back and he told me to get back in the hospital. My fever was up to 105 degrees again.

Doctors ran more tests. Three days passed. Wasn't nothing I could do and I wasn't getting no better. Finally a correct diagnosis came. My kidney was blown. Doctor said it was shriveled like a prune.

For the third time in not very long I had major surgery. This was the kidney that had been causing me problems since I was born, the one that had come untethered and was floating around by my stomach. They opened me up through the same scar in my abdomen where they had cut out my appendix and my uterus, and took out my kidney.

Now, I guess it ain't no small task to take out a kidney, even if it is untied, and they kept me in the hospital for two weeks all hooked up to these tubes. Then I went home. I couldn't walk at first. They told me not to do no more heavy lifting for the rest of my life, and that was okay because I wasn't lifting much of anything, and they said to drink a beer every day to keep me flushed, but I never liked the taste of beer or what it did to a body so I wasn't gonna do that. All I could do was lie in my bed. Mama came by and fed me mashed potatoes, chicken soup, black-eyed peas, and steamed rice. It took two months before I felt good enough to go back to work at the glass factory.

Bills was piling up but we was getting by. Money was much tighter than it had been for some time—and it was always tight, even at the best of times. Paying a mortgage took so much more than what rent was in the projects. Funny how your problems can be caught up by your children even when you want so bad for them not to know. I never talked about money problems to the boys. I figured they didn't need to know those things. Here I was thinking it was all a secret, locked up inside of me like so much else I was feeling, but one day after school Reginald came home and I could tell he was feeling down. I had got a call that day from school that I needed to ask him about too. He came into my room where I was lying.

"What's the matter, son?" I asked.

"It ain't nothing, Mama," he said.

I put my hand on his forehead. It felt cool. "School called today. They said you was sick."

"Yessum. I didn't feel well at all today."

"Today was your big field trip to the planetarium, wasn't it? You been talking about it all week."

"Yessum."

"So you didn't go on your field trip, then?"

"No ma'am." Reginald lowered his head. "I didn't."

"They said you was standing in front of the principal's office saying you was sick. Then you spent the day at the nurse's office. Is that true?"

"Yessum."

"Are you truly sick then?"

"No ma'am, not really."

"So how come you lied to the school?"

Reginald squirmed. There was no look of withholding truth from me, just a sad look on his face and I could see the corners of his mouth quivering. I decided to ask the question again, phrased a little different this time: "How come you told the school you was sick and kept yourself from going to the planetarium?"

"Because," Reginald said. Then he let loose with his heart a bit and one tear rolled down his cheek. "I told them I was sick because I didn't want to put no pressure on you, Mama."

"What do you mean by that?"

"It cost two dollars to get in the planetarium, Mama. And I knowed you didn't have it. I didn't know how I was gonna get the money, so that's why I told them I was sick and stayed back at school. I didn't know what else to do."

I held my son to me for a long while. I stroked the back of his head. My brave son. The pain was all mine now. What did I ever do to deserve boys like this?

I was determined more than ever to never let my boys down again. I would never get sick no more. I would never be missing no more work. They was depending on me. I had my strength back nearly and I had my resolve, and nothing was gonna push me off the road upward that we was on. Absolutely nothing.

8

What Stopped Me

NOTHING FELT DIFFERENT ABOUT THIS particular evening.

It wasn't the weekend yet.

It was during the week.

I looked at the clock over the door of the H.L. Green five-and-dime store as I walked outside and saw it was a few minutes after 6 P.M.

Not late yet. Not late by any means.

My boys were over at my mama's, their safe headquarters.

I was doing a little shopping by myself.

Folks milled in and out of the store.

Like they always do.

Wasn't many folks out that night.

Don't know why there wasn't many folks.

Wish there had been more folks.

More folks can hear you scream.

Walking toward the bus stop, I had a package under my arm.

H&L was downtown.

The bus stop to get back to Sheridan Heights was around the corner and down the street a spell.

From where I was I could still see the lights from the H.L. Green sign.

I couldn't tell you what kind of car it was.

A Maverick or a Chevelle or a Nova. It don't matter now.

It pulled over next to me and stopped.

Music blared from the AM radio in the dash.

Wailing guitars. Raspy, screaming singer.

With the music came a lull,

a second or two of pure lull.

You don't know what to do.

You're just trying to figure out what's going on.

Then everything sped up—

The driver lunged from his door and ran around at me and shouted something I couldn't understand. His passenger-side door flew open and his hands pushed me and I wasn't moving but he was shoving hard and I said I didn't want no ride nowhere but he heaved me inside his car and slammed the door and it wouldn't open from the inside and I didn't know this man from no one: Why didn't no one hear me scream or hear his tires squeal or smell them smoke as he gunned the motor or why didn't someone say, "Hey that driver's gonna kill someone driving like that," and think to call the police? We was flying now and weaving in and out of traffic and I thought for sure we was gonna hit a light post or the back of another car. He smelled like underarm and whiskey and that ugly tang of pot smoke, and this crazy music still blared from the radio and the pounding hurt my head. My mouth was open from shock and I clutched at the door handle frantically trying to open it but he wasn't slowing down neither and I didn't want to fly out of the car and bounce off the curb. "You want my purse?" I said. "Take it! Just take it!" He grabbed my purse with one hand and held the wheel with the other. "Shut up!" he snarled. "You don't say nothing!" We sped through the streets and he rummaged through my purse and grabbed out my wallet and shoved the bills in his shirt pocket and threw my purse in the backseat and all the while he didn't slow down and his car careened down the road and we approached the highway. "Where you taking me?" I said. He reached inside his coat pocket and pulled out a revolver, one of those black pistols you only see in movies, and waved the gun at me: "I got a knife too! So shut up, bitch! You shut the f— up, or I'm gonna blow your face wide open!" It was so hard to think and I was trying so hard to think: What were my options? What were my options! I couldn't think. I couldn't think: I didn't have no options, no options at all, and we sped down the highway and the city was behind us and he made a sharp turn and the tires squealed again and we flew off the main road and everything was dark and there were no other cars and I saw a wooded area and thick trees and I decided to speak again although my mouth was dry: "Where we going?" I croaked it out and I didn't recognize my voice but it was all I could think to say: Maybe if I had some sort of bearing I could think of something to do, but he smacked the gun down hard on the dash and it's a wonder it didn't go off and he was screaming now really screaming: "Shut up! Shut up! Shut up! I said I don't want to hear your voice, bitch! You shut the f— up!" Then he slammed on the brakes and my head cracked the windshield and we jolted to a stop and dust was rising through the car and exhaust was all around us and everything was smoke and noise and he was over at my door now unlocking it pulling it open yanking me out shoving me down tripping me kicking at my legs throwing me on the ground. The back of my head thudded on the dirt: "What are you doing?" I said and I begged: "Leave me alone leave me alone please leave me alone for God's sake leave me alone." I was wearing a jacket and a blouse and pants and he straddled me, the long bowie knife flashed in his hands, and he started slashing at my clothes and ripping buttons and tearing at the fabric. "You must want it real bad," he said, and that was the last thing he said, and in a frenzy I exploded and clawed his face and scratched and bit and kicked and he was hitting me now and slashing my arms with his knife and his hands went around my neck and the air was choked tight within me and I couldn't exhale or draw breath in and he slammed my head back against the dirt with his hands still clutching my throat and I started to black out and found that I couldn't fight back as much anymore and he let go of my neck with one hand and started cutting at me again with his knife and he slashed at my thighs and Satan jabbed his way into me—rushing down and swooping in as the angel of darkness himself—and I felt my flesh shredding and I saw Jesus hanging alongside me twisting on the cross with his arms jerked out of his sockets with spikes through his hands and thorns through his brow and Jesus was bearing the full fury of Hades within his body, and that same hell was all upon me now, all the demons that ever walked the earth: I was in their midst, shrieking forth vomit and terror and horror. My God! Why have you forsaken me? My God! My God! I never stopped resisting. I never stopped. The devil kept hitting me when he was inside of me: He kept hitting me, then he grunted and finished and climbed to standing and kicked me and dirt showered upon me and I lay exposed. The car's tires spun again. They spun grass and dust, and I was on the ground by myself alone.

Trees towered above me. I could see that much in the dark. My neck was on fire. My body was broken. I gathered my clothes about me as best I could and tried to stand.

What was I supposed to do now?

Just what?

I didn't see no lights.

No houses or stores.

I tried calling out but no one heard me.

I stumbled forward, putting one foot ahead of the other.

Walking somewhere. Anywhere.

I didn't know what else to do. So I walked.

Don't know how long I walked.

After some time a police car found me.

At first they wanted to know what I was doing out there all alone.

Then they musta looked closer at me with their flashlights because their tones changed real sudden and they was helping me sit down and giving me a blanket and asking me if there was anybody I wanted them to call for me.

The backseat of the police cruiser felt cool to my forehead as they drove me to the station.

Then there were bright lights and they asked me to sit down on a hardback seat and I heard the clatter of a typewriter and a policeman was asking me questions and there was a book of mug shots in front of me and they had me leaf through the book but all the faces blurred together and I didn't want to remember this man's face.

Georgia and Rosa came to the station to get me.

My sisters.

They brought me a change of clothes.

The police kept my other clothes as evidence.

Then Georgia and Rosa drove me to the hospital.

There was more bright lights there.

Stitches.

Ice.

Doctors. Nurses were coming in and going out and a sea of voices and noises were around me and I felt myself sinking, sinking.

A light was down the corridor from me and I walked toward it.

The light was red and said EXIT.

That's what I want to do.

Then I was outside. In the backseat of my sister's car.

My eyes closed.

The heater must have been on because I was feeling hot and my forehead was wet and so was my cheeks.

I didn't want to talk to nobody and I musta convinced my sisters that I'd be all right, and I didn't tell them much that happened anyway.

Then I was inside my bathroom and my door was locked tight and the water to the shower was pouring forth and it was as hot as I could stand it and the steam was rising and I was scrubbing with the soap and I dumped the whole bottle of shampoo over my head and I was using a washcloth and there wasn't enough soap—there just wasn't enough soap—and I climbed out and stood on the cold bathroom tiles while I dripped all over and the hot water kept running and I found another bar of soap and unwrapped it and climbed back in the shower with the new bar of soap and I wasn't coming clean, I just wasn't coming clean.

How many hours passed?

My boys musta spent the night at my mama's house because the next morning they wasn't there with me.

I didn't go to work.

Didn't even call in to tell them I was sick.

Don't know how long I stayed away from work but after a while I went back.

They put a small article in the newspaper.

They never put my name in the article.

That was the last I heard of the incident.

Mama came over.

Mama.

She fed me scalloped potatoes with lots of cheese just like I like it. That's what I remember. Those scalloped potatoes tasted real good.

After that I just wanted to lie down even though it might have been the middle of the day.

And whenever I did my eyes closed and I saw shapes and swirls and folks' faces and I heard voices and laughing.

And other folks might be in a room with me and talking to me but I was just sitting on a couch looking at a corner in the ceiling because that's the only place it felt safe to look.

And maybe I was just imagining those other folks there in the room with me after all.

9

So Much Bad

THAT'S WHAT I WANTED TO forget.

Forget. Forget. Forget.

Mama went with me to the hospital for the shock treatments. Somebody else drove. Mama didn't drive. She never did. I couldn't tell you who drove. Daddy didn't drive neither. Maybe it was one of my older sisters or brothers. Everything was blurry in my mind. All I saw was the black back of someone's head in the front seat while Mama sat close to me in the back. Maybe it was winter. Or maybe it was spring. It didn't matter much to me. The building loomed up big and white in front of us as the car drove into the circular driveway. Then we was under a large awning with skylights, I think, because shafts of glowing came down around us like spotlights. The car's door handle felt cold as I closed the door behind me. It was strangely chilled for Alabama's usual heat. Mama took my arm and we started walking although I felt like sitting. A smile crossed my face as the doors opened for us. I wanted to be here.

I don't quite know how much time had passed since the rape. It might have been months. It might have been a year. It might have been longer. I wasn't keeping track of time just then. I was on again off again at work. And I was taking a heap of pills. That was for sure. Couldn't exactly tell you all the pills I was taking. There was therapy too and a lot of talk but nothing was doing much for the misery I felt inside. Mostly I was just crying. Crying. Crying. Crying. I was going to work and crying and coming home from work and crying and lying on the couch at home and crying. That was my life and I knowed it wasn't no way to live. So that's when I decided it would be good for me to go to Jackson Hospital and have those treatments.

Doctors were real hopeful that the shock treatments would do something for me. Sometimes the treatments worked real wonders when folks had real bad depression. But when those treatments were over they didn't do nothing for me. Some things I wanted so badly to forget, and some things I was fighting to remember too. When the shock treatments was over I could remember everything, both the good and the bad, and there was so much bad I was feeling just then. So much bad.

It was that next day after I had hallucinated about Uncle Roosevelt wanting to stop by my hospital room that Mama came and got me. She signed me out of the hospital and we went home to her house. She propped me up on the couch in her living room and went into the kitchen to cook. That's when I slept for once. Sleep felt good but you gotta wake up sometime and I did, and I still felt miserable then too. All the horrible stuff kept running through my mind. I wanted it out of my mind but none of it would leave. I didn't know where to turn or who to talk to. After the shock treatments there wasn't no place left I could turn, I figured. So that's when I started figuring that there was only one thing left to do.

"Mama," I called from the couch. "I'm feeling a bit better this morning. I'm gonna go back home to my house." I rubbed the sleep out of my eyes.

Mama came in from the kitchen where she was dishing up breakfast. "You sure, Martha? I don't know if you should leave just yet."

"Yeah, I'm feeling real good today," I said. I hoped Mama wouldn't discern the lie from my lips.

So I went home. I was a grown-up. What could Mama do if she disagreed? No one was at my home when I walked through the front door. Everything was just how I left it. The sofa. The TV. The same carpet. The same middle-class house on Faro Drive. The boys musta been at school. Daddy musta been looking after them, I guessed. Some particulars I wasn't asking about. They were just being handled for me, and that was fine with me for sure.

A stomachache was coming on so I walked to my bathroom and opened the cupboard underneath the sink. I kept my big bag of medicines in there. There was lots of tiny bottles and some bigger bottles too. They all rolled around together in my big medicine bag. I felt like having some pills just then. Yes sir. I really did. My stomach was hurting and now my head was hurting too. Some pills would be just the ticket.

Strange, real strange. As I was fishing in my medicine bag looking for the right bottle I felt something in the bathroom with me. I didn't quite know what it was, or who it was, but it was some sort of company that had showed up. A type of otherworldly houseguest, or a lot of houseguests maybe, I don't rightly know. I couldn't make out exactly what the feeling was for sure and a shiver ran down my back that made me not want to look in the mirror for fear I'd see something that wasn't my own face.

I didn't like the idea of something being in my bathroom with me. Still, the more minutes that ticked by, the more it felt like kindly company. Maybe things would be all right with it being there. What could I do about it, anyway? It was probably all in my mind. I reached for a big bottle of pills then nearly jumped out of my skin when the company spoke: "Martha," it said. "You're so tired." I glanced all around the bathroom. How did it know my name? I couldn't see nothing there. Now I knowed I was crazy for sure. The company kept speaking: "You've been through so much, Martha. You need to be good to yourself for a change." I looked into the bag of medicines. They'd help me sort out what was real.

There was one pill I was supposed to take every day. That pill felt so good when it was inside my head. Now, what pill was it again? "It's the blue pill in the large bottle." I heard the company say. It was being helpful. "That's the one you want to take." I swallowed the blue pill, set down the medicine bag, and walked to the living room.

That's when the mental dominoes started. Sitting down proved a problem. If I sat I started to think. And I didn't want to think. Not then. But I had had too much sleep the night before on my mama's couch and I wasn't sleepy in my living room and I made the mistake of sitting so that's when the dominoes started. You push over one domino in your head and the next one drops. Then it's a chain of thoughts that start to fall, one after the next: What was I gonna do? How was I ever gonna feel better? When was things ever gonna feel normal again? One by one the thoughts fell. Then the company spoke again. Sure enough it was sitting right next to me in the living room. It asked a question I didn't expect: "Martha—remember when you were too poor to have an inside bathroom?"

I nodded. I didn't know why the company was asking me questions about my past. I didn't want to remember my past. Sure enough the questions kept coming. "Not much good comes from being so poor, does it?" the company said. "Not much good at all."

I nodded again. The words were coming slowly, rhythmically, hypnotically.

"Here's something else to think about—" the company said. "You don't have blond hair, do you? . . . Isn't it true that only pretty girls have blond hair?"

Now why would the company ask about my hair? I reached up and felt the top of my head. The last shower I had taken had been two days earlier when I was still at Jackson hospital. My hair felt dirty and matted. It's true. I was ugly.

The voice continued: "You've made some . . ." this next word was chosen carefully, I could tell, " . . . *interesting* decisions in your life, haven't you, Martha? You remember what happened when you were with Reuben . . . Then came Sylvester . . . And then came James . . . They all left you, didn't they, Martha. Tell me—why is no one ever there for you, Martha?"

I shook my head. That company was starting to make sense. Too much sense. I didn't know why no one was ever there for me. I felt my bottom lip quivering and tears were coming on.

"Well, there's one person who's here for you, Martha," the company's voice said. I was craning my ears to hear who it was. The voice sounded so warm. So compelling. Its next words came quietly: "I'm the only one who's here for you, Martha . . . I'm the only one who cares for *you*."

Just like that the company was gone. Was that a laugh I heard right at the end? It couldn't be a laugh because nothing was funny. But it sure sounded like a laugh, so I wasn't sure what I heard. My tongue was tingling. I could feel it trembling. Was it because I was crying? And why did my tongue feel so strange? A million tiny nerve endings were buzzing inside my mouth. I tried to swallow but the spit wouldn't go down. Something was pushing my teeth apart. It was coming right out of my mouth. My tongue felt like an inner tube attached to an air pump, and someone was working the pump hard. I was starting to gag. I opened my mouth and tried to push my tongue back in. It wouldn't go back in. It was getting harder to breathe. The buzzing was coursing through the rest of my body. An arm flailed one way. A leg went another. Everything started to shake. I wanted to stand up, to run to the phone and call for help, but my arms and legs wouldn't cooperate. Sharp pains jabbed the right side of my gut, my neck, my head. My whole body started thrashing.

Jerking. Jerking. Jerking. I was biting on a balloon, gasping for air. Jerking. Jerking. Jerking.

Then came blackness. Emptiness. Nothing was there in the void of blacking out that I could see. Nothing was there but the company. I couldn't see it but it spoke to me with the same hypnotic voice: "Is this really the way you want to spend the rest of your life, Martha?" One little phrase. That phrase jerked around my body and buzzed and zapped and jolted and tried to get out. That was all.

Then I was in the emergency room. I don't know how I got there. I don't know who found me blacked out at home. Mama was at the doctor's office with me. She was using a wet towel and dabbing my mouth with it. The towel felt cool on my lips and swollen tongue. I could breathe a bit easier. The doctor gave me a shot. "You'll be all right in a couple hours, Martha," the doctor said. "Just lie down and it will pass soon."

Turns out that the blue pill I had taken had a nasty habit of producing some side effects. That's what the tongue swelling and seizures was all about. The doctor made some adjustments and after that I was supposed to take another smaller pill before I took the blue pill. But that sounded hard to keep straight. Why would anyone think you could remember that when you're not in your right mind in the first place? The doctor was clear that he still wanted me to keep taking that blue pill—but just be more careful!—that's what he said.

Then I was back at my house and back in my own bed. Don't know how I got there neither. I saw darkness and light then darkness and light. Days musta been passing. Days. Days. Lots of days passed and I let them go by. All I wanted to do was sleep.

After a while I felt okay enough so I went back to work then I came home. Then another week passed. Maybe it was a month. Folks was coming and going and I must have been talking to them enough because I saw my sons from day to day. They was going to school and not causing no problems, Mama, they said to me. They had got together as boys and had a meeting even: they wasn't putting no pressure on me ever, they decided among themselves. They just wanted me to get well soon. That was what they wanted. I liked it when they said that.

I had some good days when the company musta left for the day because it wasn't around. But on the bad days, boy, that company had some nerve.

One day when I was doing a lot of crying that company came right into my bedroom with me. I sure didn't want nothing in my bedroom with me. The company's voice had more force to it this time. "I want you to get up and go to your bathroom," the company said. So I did. Strange what you'll do when somebody's telling you what to do, and that company could be mighty persuasive. "I want you to open the cupboard with your medicines and get out the bag," the company said. So I did. The voice was still friendly. Still low. "Take out the bottles and line them up in front of you, Martha." And I did. "This will help you," the company said, and I heard water splashing into the sink. I had a glass with me and I filled it with water. The dominoes were starting to drop in my mind again. Don't know who pushed over the first one: Poor Martha. Always something bad happening to her. Bad relationships. Getting sick. Going to the hospital. No money. Never being able to have a normal life. Everything always so painful. If you got to hurt like this so much of the time you don't know how you're ever gonna keep going. That's what I was thinking now. The dominoes were falling faster.

That first pill felt so good inside my head when I washed it down with water. The second pill slid down easy in my brain too. Then it was a handful of pills floating inside me. Lots of pills. I lost track of how many pills I took. That's what I wanted to do: lose track. Then I turned the water off. There was no more water left in my glass neither. I wandered to my bedroom, lay down, and pulled the covers over my head. I wondered how long it would take before I wouldn't be hurting no more. I just couldn't bear no more pain any longer. I just couldn't.

Folks musta figured I was real tired because I just stayed in my bed at home and slept. There was daylight and darkness then daylight then darkness. When the daylight came to me for the third time I didn't want to reach for that daylight. It was three days after my overdose and I woke up feeling weepy and groggy. I could hardly move. Obviously I hadn't taken enough pills to do the job right.

"Mmmm, too bad. Another failure for you," the company said. It was the first voice I heard after waking up. I shook my head like you do when you shake water out of your ears and tried to get the company to quit talking. I didn't want it to be the first voice I heard but it was speaking real loudly this time. "Better try again," it said. "Better try again right now." My shoulders slumped. The company was probably right. Pretty soon I was standing in my bathroom again reaching for another bottle of pills, but this time I heard someone else in the living room and this person was real.

Nyrone, my youngest. He was here in the house with me. Nyrone was old enough to be left alone, I guess, left alone with me while everybody thought his mama was sleeping. I glanced at the clock. What was Nyrone doing home from school at this time of day? With my son here it felt like I should do something. But what should I do? I wandered into the kitchen and thought about making some banana pudding. The pudding wasn't sounding good to me to eat it, but I needed to do something with my hands and banana pudding was what came to mind. I always made real good banana pudding. Nyrone would like that. But my body wasn't working right. Nothing wanted to move very quick. I had to talk myself through each step in the process and consciously tell my body to take each action: go to fridge and get out some milk; set the jug of milk on the counter, let go of the milk jug with your hand; open the cupboard and take out the sugar.

Cupboard?

That made me remember the cupboard under my bathroom sink, the cupboard with all the medicine in it. I didn't want to go into the bathroom and look inside the cupboard. I truly didn't want to. But it was such a strong compulsion telling me it would be a good thing if I did. My mind fought itself. The things I didn't want to do, I was pretty sure I was gonna do them. The things I wanted to do, those were the things I wasn't gonna do. The company was speaking again. It was telling me everything would be okay if I did go into the bathroom. I was just gonna look at my bag of medicine—that was all. Maybe I was just gonna peek inside the bag then put it back. Things would surely be okay if all I did was peek.

I set down the banana pudding and started walking to the bathroom. Dominoes started again. The first one was pushed over real quick this time: Yes. Do this. Do this right this time. This is the answer you're was looking for. Your sons would be so much better off with you not being a part of their lives. Your mama could take your place and do a much better job raising them. You're gonna feel better really soon.

All that sounded so good.

But wait! I needed to get rid of Nyrone first. He couldn't be in the house when this was happening.

Don't know what I said to Nyone. Don't know what he said to me. But there we was in my Pinto together and I was driving Nyrone over to my mama's house. Don't know what I said to Mama neither. And don't know why I took Nyrone over there and not to school. Don't know what Mama said to me neither and I don't know how I convinced her that I was okay to be alone just then. But soon enough I was back at my house with no one around and this time I walked straight to my bathroom with no argument from no one.

So this was it.

The water came on clear and cold and it rushed into the sink and down the drain. I crouched down and fished around in the cupboard and peeked into the bag of medicine. There was still plenty of pills there. Dominoes were racing now, falling like bricks being thrown off a roof. Nothing mattered. I had a life that didn't have no meaning. Nobody would ever love me. I was always gonna be stupid and ugly. There was always gonna be another problem around each corner. Wasn't no way out but this. One by one the dominoes were hurled to the ground. I lined up the bottles on the counter. Everything was hurting so bad. My head hurt. My stomach hurt. My heart hurt. If I could just stop hurting for a while, then things would be okay. Wouldn't they? Wouldn't they?

"Yes, they will," the company said. "Everything will stop hurting soon, Martha. This is exactly what you need to do. There is no other way than this." The company was always showing up at the crucial time. If I had any doubts left, the company's words were all the prompting I needed. I uncapped the bottle in my hand and began to swallow pills. I swallowed and swallowed. I swallowed pills until I thought I couldn't swallow no more. The water was still rushing down the sink. I'd just leave it on. Empty brown pill bottles covered my bathroom floor. I wasn't making no mistakes this time.

A few seconds before I blacked out I thought I heard something. I couldn't see straight no longer but I swear I heard laughing. I was lying on the floor and something was sitting on my chest and I couldn't breathe much, and I didn't want to breathe really, and this long cackling laughter was running through the bathroom and it was coming from the thing that was sitting on my chest.

I recognized the company for who he was now. The company wasn't talking to me no more with his sweet, warm words. He was laughing at me for me being so stupid. He was laughing because he was holding my hand tight, and I was letting him, and his hand was as cold as a corpse. As I lay on the bathroom floor with a bag of pills inside my body he was taking me to hell with him. That's why the company was laughing, for that's where it had come from in the first place.

IO

A Single Light

THEY CAN STICK A TUBE through your mouth if you're still conscious. But I guess it's much easier to go through your nose because it don't trigger your gag reflex that way. The strength of the suction can be fiddled with and there's no time limit involved: they just pump and pump until all the junk in your stomach runs clear. Then they give you charcoal to eat because it soaks up any poison that might be still floating around your system. As a side effect, the charcoal arouses your bowels something fierce and everything runs out of you. It ain't pretty, but that's how you get your stomach pumped. That's what they told me anyway, after that's what was done for me. When your stomach pumping is over they bring in a psych consult to figure out why you wanted to kill yourself in the first place. But I wasn't talking too much just yet.

Daddy and my uncle Ollie had found me. Mama had instructed them to rush over. What had tipped her off all right was when I had brought Nyrone to her house and not to school. That made her call Daddy and Uncle Ollie and they came over and rang the doorbell at my house, and then kicked in the back door because they knowed somebody was home. I was passed out cold on my bathroom floor.

An ambulance had rushed me to the hospital. This time it was either Jackson, where I had once had the shock treatments, or Baptist Hospital, I don't rightly remember, because I wasn't at this particular hospital for long. Very soon they sent me to Greil on the Upper Wetumpka Road. That was okay by me. Don't know what else I was gonna do except go to a place like Greil. The full name was Greil Memorial Psychiatric Hospital, but nobody was politically correct back then and we all just knowed it as the loony bin. Greil is your last stop. It's where you go when you don't have no hope left on the outside. You either make it at Greil and get busy living, or you don't make it and fade away—'cause that's all that's left for you to do.

With all the meds pumped out of my stomach I was seeing things more clearly, and as we drove up to Greil I noticed it was a quiet place made up of low, flat brick buildings surrounded by lawns and shrubs that were sure to bud and flower sometime soon. The bricks ran along the building walls and there was a high ribbon of white stucco along the top. Greil had been built only a few years back, in 1974. For a place of last resort, in my thinking, it looked almost pretty.

Inside, the floor was tiled and new, sort of a green-and-white pattern. I was looking at that tile floor when they brought me in the entryway. A receptionist was behind a glass partition, which I saw when I glanced up. She said hello all friendly-like and asked me a bunch of questions and handed me some papers though someone else filled them out for me. Then the receptionist unlocked the inside doors and I shuffled down the hallway to where I was to stay.

Me and my brothers and sisters helped celebrate my parents' fiftieth wedding anniversary in 1976. *Sitting, left to right:* Georgia Jackson, Alice Peterson, Alberta Woodson, Sallie B. Hawkins (my mama), me, Willela Dawson, Rosalee Williams. *Standing, left to right:* Henry Harvest (my uncle), Henry Hawkins, Willie Jr., Willie Sr. (my daddy), Tommy, Edward, Howard, Scott, Willie C. Hawkins (my uncle).

Christopher Reeve spoke at an event for the Eli Lilly Company in Washington, D.C., where I received an award. I'm second from the right, standing next to Darold Dunlavy from the Montgomery Mental Health Association, who nominated me for the award.

Actor Clifton Davis and me.
We catered an event for him.

Nell Carter and me, hanging out
in the restaurant.

Ted Koppel enjoyed pork chop
casserole and collards. He was
filming a *Nightline* episode in
Montgomery and stopped by for
some authentic soul food.

I always enjoy speaking to high school students. This group came down from North Carolina.

Me speaking at a women's event.

Three of the boys and me, 1981.
Shawn had just begun college and wasn't around for the photo.
Clockwise from me: Nyrone, Quintin, Reginald.

Family reunion. *Back row, left to right:* Krista and Reggie;
Brianna, Nyrone, and Yolanda; Sharon, Quint, and Natalyn.
Front, left to right: Gabrielle, me, Shawn, and Martina.
(Christian, Carsyn, and Nyia weren't born yet.)

Nyrone (my youngest) and his wife, Yolanda, today.

Me with my parents in their front yard in Sheridan Heights.

Top: My boys and their wives today. *Left to right:* Quint and Natalyn, Nyrone and Yolanda, me, Krista and Reggie, Sharon and Shawn.

Bottom: My whole family today. *Left to right:* Quint and Natalyn with Christian and Carsyn, Nyrone and Yolanda holding Nyia, me, Brianna with Reginald and Krista, Martina, Gabrielle, Sharon, Shawn.

Ty Pennington and the team from *Extreme Makeover: Home Edition* stopped by the restaurant and enjoyed corn bread, collards, and fried chicken. Later, Ty ordered some more food from the restaurant while out on the shoot.

Shawn, Nyrone, me, and Reginald at the Eli Lilly awards in Washington, D.C. (Quint was back in Montgomery taking care of the restaurant.)

Doug McMillion, president and CEO of Wal-Mart International, and me. He is truly a great man.

Shawn shaking hands with President George H. W. Bush.

Somebody said they had a hundred beds at Greil, and I felt relieved it wasn't a really big place. For a state mental ward everything looked sane to me—no bars on the windows or nothing. It just looked like the inside of a hospital building with rooms and nurses and a common area in the middle they called the activity room. I could see other patients milling about in the activity room when they walked me to my room. But they sent a shiver through me so I averted my glance from their direction. I was more comfortable staring at the floor.

A nurse told me that during the first two weeks at Greil nobody was allowed to come see me. That was fine 'cause I wasn't in no shape to be talking, although I was thinking about my boys and wondering if they was okay. In moments when I was able to sift through the last bit of time, I knew something was real wrong with me. I didn't know how to fix things, that was for sure, and that was the scariest part. I had given up hope of things ever getting fixed. That's why I had tried to kill myself.

The first day went by at Greil pretty quiet, and then another. The doctors play with your meds at first, trying to figure out the right doses. There's a heap of antipsychotic meds a person can take and most take time to kick in. Another factor is that some meds work for some folks but not for others, so doctors need to experiment with you for a while to get the particulars right. The first meds they give you after any crisis are to sedate you, they call it being calmed down. Mostly I felt like crying, so that's what I did those first few days at Greil. I was supposed to be going to meetings as soon as I felt able and talking at the meetings, but I wasn't set to be doing no talking yet. Mostly I lay in my bed and tried to sleep, even if it was the middle of the day. Other times I ate the lunches or suppers they brought me. Other times I walked down to the activity room just to get out of my room for a while. But I didn't like the activity room much at first.

It was seeing the eyes of the other patients that made me shudder. Their eyes weren't evil. They weren't even so much sad. But so many of their eyes looked so empty, like there was a body attached to those eyes but inside nobody was home. I wasn't judging those folks. On the contrary, I was thinking my eyes probably looked the same like that. I was afraid of looking into them.

Everybody's hair was crazy, too. I don't know why that bothered me so, but everywhere I looked I saw crazy hair. It wasn't only the look of slept-on hair. It was pulled-up hair, and twisted hair, and chewed-the-ends-of hair. There were lots of nurses at Greil and I knowed they were looking after patients well because they came by my room all the time and I liked it when they did, but nurses are busy in general and it takes some time to do another person's hair right and the patients was probably messing it up soon again so I didn't fault the nurses for how everybody's hair looked. Still, all that crazy hair bothered me.

It was probably a week into my stay that I wandered out of my room one morning, a box of Kleenex in hand, and headed for the activity room. I figured I'd sit a spell and collect my thoughts. There was an orange plastic chair near a window and I sat. Across the room some distance away an older lady was sitting and darting her eyes toward me and away from me quick-like. Whenever I glanced her direction she was sizing me up. She was fine featured and wore silver-rimmed glasses and set her jaw just so. If she hadn't been in the loony bin she could have passed for royalty. After some time she shuffled over, sat in another chair about five feet away, and started looking at me out of the corners of her eyes. She was wearing a pink dressing gown with tassels on the ends of her sleeves and it looked like someone had given it to her for Christmas once because it had a tiny green wreath and a bow embroidered over the lapel. The robe was faded now, and the queenlike lady's hair was standing straight up all helter-skelter, though it didn't detract from her regality much, and she was twisting the ends of her hair with her fingers.

"I have some friends here," said the lady after a while. She didn't say it as a boast because she said it with a kindly smile, and I caught that smile right when I was glancing her way. She kept sitting where she was sitting. I turned back to my window. It might have been good for me to talk with her, I was thinking. Maybe I should say something back. But I didn't know what to say and I didn't think I could get any words out of me just then, even if I tried.

She sat maybe five minutes more without saying anything else. Then she sighed, not an annoyed sigh, but just a sigh like she was trying to think of what to say next and wanted to start the process off by clearing the air, and she said, "There's a pretty puzzle I know. I can find it on the shelf. It shows water lilies when you put it all together."

I guessed she was inviting me to make that puzzle. That was real friendly and it sounded like it would be a good thing to do. But I couldn't, I just couldn't then. The dominoes felt poised to fall in my head and I was trying so hard to push those dominoes back to a standing position. Maybe I had sat in the activity room too long for my own good. Maybe I should go back to my room where it was quieter. So that's what I started to do. I got up and shuffled around the queen in the pink Christmas robe. When I got to the door I didn't turn around to look back and see if she was still looking at me. I went to my room and lay down.

It was about the second week at Greil when the counselor said I needed to start talking or else there wasn't gonna be much use. We were sitting in a circle, maybe ten of us, and the counselor said the only way we was ever gonna get better was to talk about what was inside. She motioned to the person at her right and he began talking. It was a sorry story about a car wreck and folks dying and drinking scotch afterward. The man's voice got ruffled and he slurred his words and sometimes he said sentences real loud with a lot of nonsense words strung together like *SO EVEN WITH TRIANGULAR NOODLE YOU KNOW MOTORCYCLE BUT HE RIVER FLOW AMBER ROD.* Then a woman talked about being angry long ago at her daddy and a neighbor boy down the street, but she was sadder and quieter than the first.

We was going around in a circle and I could feel the talk coming to where I was sitting. My chest was getting tighter as the talk came to me. I really wanted to talk when it got to be my turn. I think I did anyway. But when it came to be me all I could do was start crying. That's the way things had been going for me ever since I got to Greil, but the thing different today was the counselor had said real firm that we needed to start talking, or else—and I knew that. It wasn't no ultimatum because the counselor said it all kind-like. It was more just a statement of fact—and I knew that too. Talking is what we needed to do. But I couldn't talk. Not just then. So I started crying. Then I went back to my room and lay down.

A few days after that my boys were allowed to come visit. The visit was real short. When I saw them I wanted to head down to the kitchen and cook something for them, maybe some peach cobbler or a strawberry shortcake, it was so good to see them, just so good—that's how I felt inside—but I couldn't get no words to come out of me, no words at all. I was bottled so tight. They just hugged me, and Nyrone brought me a picture he had drawn at school, and the visit was over real quick and then they was gone.

I sat for some time after that on my bed. Then came lunch and it was crackers and chicken noodle soup with little pools of fat congealed on the top, but I wasn't eating. I pushed the tray aside and stopped crying enough to wander down to the activity center where the same queenlike lady with the Christmas gown was sitting on a couch with her hair flying. I sat in a chair some distance from her. She kept looking at me again and I wanted so bad to hold her gaze and become her friend, but the window felt safer to look out of, so that's where I kept looking.

"There's a TV here," she said after a while. "Sometimes I watch TV in the afternoon."

It was a real normal thing for her to say. I wanted to watch TV with her. I wondered what shows she liked. I didn't watch much TV but sometimes at the end of a shift at the glass factory I came home and turned something on. Maybe she liked *The Bionic Woman* like I did, or maybe we could watch *The Love Boat*. Those wouldn't be on in the afternoon but maybe a repeat of *Laverne & Shirley* would be on. I always liked *Laverne & Shirley*. I wanted to say something, I really did, but I could feel myself start to cry again, and then I was full-on doing it. So I got up without saying anything and walked back to my room.

All that afternoon I cried in my room. Maybe it was from the feeling of seeing my boys that triggered this particular flow. I cried when the nurse brought in supper. It was baked chicken with rice and peas on the side and I tried a bite or two but I couldn't finish it. I was crying again that evening and I cried myself to sleep, and my dreams was all about crying. When I woke the next morning I was okay for a spell but then I went to another group meeting and when the talk came around to me I knowed I needed to say something but I started crying again and that's how it was still going when I went back to my room.

You get anxious when you're crying all the time. Your face feels all flushed and your eyes feel blurry. By my bed there was a drawer and I opened it. I don't know why exactly. Maybe I was looking for more tissue. Inside the drawer sat a Bible, one of those Gideons they put in hotels and hospitals. I didn't feel much like reading but maybe it would take my mind off the crying. I hadn't read a Bible in a long while for myself, and the boys and me hadn't been having our Friday night Bible studies since I had gotten real bad. This Bible was just a New Testament, not the Old Testament too, and I let it fall open to the middle and read whatever I found there: *Praise be to the God and Father of our Lord Jesus Christ, the Father of compassion and the God of all comfort, who comforts us in all our troubles.* The words all kind of fell out together. I could use some of that comfort. Maybe I'd keep reading.

I flipped back to the beginning to the book of Matthew. It started out real dry, just a list of names and who the father of this fella was and who the father of that fella was and so on. I nearly closed it, but then it was talking about that old story about how the Virgin Mary was pledged to Joseph but before they was married she was pregnant and everybody was mighty worried about the trouble she was in. I could see myself in that. Then baby Jesus was born in a straw manger alongside a bunch of braying donkeys and mooing cows and I knowed for sure that I wasn't crazy back when I was a child in church and figured that Jesus was just a baby who filled his diapers like any other baby I knowed. Then there was that devil King Herod trying to take Jesus' life, and I knowed that Jesus had been born into a time and place where he wasn't appreciated much, much the same as was some of the folks in Montgomery I knowed. Then Jesus was a young man and out in the desert being tempted for forty days. He wasn't eating nothing, and I knowed how that felt because when I was feeling poorly I wasn't eating much either. There Jesus was all by himself and the wily old devil was whispering lies in his ear, telling him to throw himself down off the top of the temple, just like that company had been whispering lies in my ear.

That was enough reading for then. Sleep was coming on and I wasn't crying no more. This sleep came to me easy-like, and I noticed when I woke the next morning that this sleep didn't have no wild dreams in it like it usually did. That afternoon when I went to group meeting, the talk came around the circle and there was that same old catch in my throat rising up, and when the talk came around to me I was pretty sure I was gonna start crying again because all eyes were on me. Then it flashed in my mind what I had seen the day before about how God is all about comforting us, so instead of crying I set my knuckles onto my chair as tight as I could and said, "My name's Martha, and I been feeling real poorly for a long while." That's what came out of me. That one sentence. My voice was real quiet and I was trembling inside and that was the sum total of my words. But the counselor smiled at me and nodded, and I almost smiled back—but not just yet then. Not just yet. I went back to my room and slept. Then came supper. Then some more sleeping. Then breakfast the next day. After breakfast I slept some that next morning. That's how things were going for me at Greil.

The evening after the day I talked in group for the first time I was sitting in the activity room and the queen was sitting near me in her faded Christmas robe. We wasn't saying anything to each other yet, but I was working up the courage to say hello and was just about there until another girl came along and plopped herself down right next to the queen. She was chewing gum and had clear smooth skin and was young, maybe nineteen or twenty. Her hair might have been straightened recently because it was curly, not kinky, and it probably would have fallen below her shoulders on a relaxed day except that this day it was wild and standing straight up.

"It's a good thing you weren't here ten years ago," the girl said straightaway. She talked quickly in that high snarly tone that black women sometimes get. "Ten years ago was before Wyatt. And Wyatt changed everything." She smacked her gum and gave her head a shake like I was a plumb idiot for not knowing who Wyatt was. "I'm gonna be a lawyer someday and I'm gonna finish Wyatt— 'cause it ain't all through yet. That's what I'm gonna do. Don't think I ain't, because I'm gonna be a lawyer for sure. I was in college once, you know."

I didn't know how to begin to answer her. I found myself rising to head back to my room and was almost standing when the queen spoke up suddenly, her hand open and upturned toward the new girl. "Water lilies are gentle, Roshanda. Real gentle. Water lilies just blow in the breeze. I like those water lilies that blow in the breeze." It was quite a mouthful for the queen. She nodded at the girl, smiled, then spoke the next phrase to me: "I have friends here, you know. Roshanda is my friend."

I got what she meant and sat back down. If the gum-chewing girl had won the queen's endorsement then she couldn't be all that bad. Roshanda stared at me, her elbow draped over the back of her chair. She blew a bubble, popped it, then leaned forward and jumped into the conversation again. "*Wyatt versus Stickney*, 1971. It's a court case right here in Alabama. I told you I was gonna be a lawyer. Wyatt changed everything. Ricky Wyatt. He was only fifteen and nuts, just like everybody here." She motioned around the room. "Ricky was housed over at Bryce, the big nuthouse over in Tuscaloosa. It was originally built for two hundred patients. But that was a hundred years ago, and by the time poor old Ricky Wyatt came along they had five thousand nutballs crammed into Bryce. Think about that—and only three shrinks, too—ha! For all those folks. None of those nutballs ever took a bath. None of 'em ever ate. Poop and pee was all over the floor. Like I said, it's a good thing you wasn't here ten years ago because they would have stuck you in at Bryce with poor old Ricky Wyatt and tied your hands to a chair just like they did to him." Roshanda grinned and looked triumphant. It was clear she wanted me to acknowledge her facts about things. I felt obliged and grabbed hold of my chair. I could do this.

"Uh . . ." I began. "I . . . I don't rightly know what to say." It was the second thing I had said in two days. One more complete sentence out of me. Yep. I was making real progress.

"You're lucky, girl, real lucky." Roshanda lunged in again. "You're in the midst of a real revolution and don't even know it. Folks think civil rights are just for us colored folks, but we got our rights too—us folks in here, I mean. And we're receiving our rights, too. Three squares a day. Hot showers anytime we want. Nice nurses. Plenty of doctors. That's right—we're receiving our rights now." Her voice rose and she waved a finger. "I might be in here with all you nutballs but I'm just as good as anybody on the outside. Why shouldn't we all have rights just like anyone else?"

I shrugged, again not sure how to respond. The queen was smiling but holding the sides of her head like too much information was floating about. I stood to leave. This time there was no stopping me.

"You just think about that, girl!" Roshanda called as I began to walk away. "You was nothing ten years ago. Before Wyatt we was all nothing! All of us nutballs in here! We was nothing!"

I didn't doubt that Roshanda was correct on her assessment of the state mental health care system—things had been bad in the system for a while, but they was getting good again, all thanks to a very recent court case. I was thankful for that, but I couldn't listen anymore. I needed to find someplace quieter.

Back in my room, I shut the door. The Bible was there on the bedside table where I had left it. I picked it up and began to read again. This time Jesus was talking with a Samaritan woman while they was sitting at a well. His disciples had all gone someplace else and it was just him and the woman. He was talking to her all calm and quiet. Not angry, though there might have been sense to him being angry as there was plenty of evil to be riled up against in his day.

As I kept reading I could tell this Samaritan woman was trying to duck out the back door from talking to Jesus. She had been through five husbands already and she knowed in her heart that wasn't okay. I could relate to having a string of men in my life just like that Samaritan woman. But Jesus wasn't bashing on her for any of that mess. He just kept talking to her, telling her a time was coming when things was gonna be okay. I liked the sound of that. I needed more people to tell me things was gonna be okay. I kept reading whenever I could.

Then about a month into my stay at Greil I opened myself up to the group. It happened one afternoon. Folks around the circle seemed to be listening to me so I just kept saying one sentence after another. It felt okay, you know. I wasn't quite sure if all my sentences was making sense, but I talked about growing up in the projects, about Reuben, about Sylvester and James. That was as far as I got, up to that point. I couldn't go much farther. Not yet. It felt good to talk.

That evening I went to the activity room and Roshanda and the queen were sitting on a couch watching TV. I had been seeing them most every day. The queen rarely said much except a sentence or two about the puzzle she kept making but she smiled whenever she saw me and I was getting to where I could almost smile back at her. Roshanda was always full of loud talk and sometimes it came out all jumbled in a word salad, but usually when you listened closely you could discern that she was a smart girl and her loud talk didn't bother me much after a while.

"I've got schizophrenia, you know," Roshanda confided to me later that evening. It was during a commercial break halfway through *Love Boat*. "You got to watch yourself in your late teens and early twenties because that's when your brain is rewiring itself and when you usually get schizophrenia." Her sentences were sounding reasoned, though her voice had a faraway sound. "I was at college doing fine, holding down a part-time job in a law office. I was doing really good—even had a boyfriend—ooooh, girl, he was fine." Roshanda smiled a dirty grin, then lowered her eyebrows and a dark look came over her face. "All my professors were out to get me. They didn't like what I was saying in class. Too off topic, they said. Well, la-di-da! Then my roommate got in on the conspiracy. I know she was stealing from me. Always touching my stuff. So I just had to quit. Quit college. Quit my job. They were planting bugs in the walls—top secret surveillance bugs—I knowed they was trying to spy on me. I wasn't gonna put up with no more spying so I kicked in a wall, trying to get those bugs out of there. That's when my boss called the cops on me. They brought me here." Her face sank as she said the last words.

Things were getting too intense. I needed to leave. Still, I wanted to be there to listen to Roshanda's story, I really did. Folks were listening to me talk, so I wanted to be there for folks when they talked. I figured that was only fair. It was nearly time for *Love Boat* to come back on. I figured I could make it. I tried my best to stay seated and not run back to my room.

"Don't ever think you won't need a nuthouse," Roshanda said. Her voice was all out of gas this time. "All of us in here—I bet none of us ever thought we'd ever need a nuthouse." She looked around the room. "We was all normal once."

Gopher and Captain Merrill Stubing came back on TV and Roshanda grew quiet. The queen hadn't taken her eyes off the TV all this time. I figured that was enough listening for one day. I hadn't been feeling the dominoes fall in my head for a while but I was scared they might again soon. I stood up to go. Roshanda kept quiet. I wanted to say something encouraging to her, I really did, I wanted to tell her things was gonna be okay. But I couldn't think of any of the words that mattered. I placed my hand on Roshanda's arm for a moment and she didn't move. I decided to quit while I was ahead and go back to my room.

Just before I left I remembered seeing a full Bible, not just a New Testament, on the shelf in the activity room when I had walked in. I spotted it anew, tucked it under my arm, and headed down the hall. This one was an old King James, a red leather edition. Someone from the outside must have dropped it off that day because most everything in Greil was new. The Bible's leather was frayed and the gold around the page edges was uneven. I set the Bible down on my bed and opened it at random. Where do you start reading a whole Bible? It fell open to the book of Isaiah. I couldn't remember ever hearing a sermon from Isaiah because I had no idea who he was or what that particular book was about.

The top of the page said chapter 61 and I read the first verse: *The Spirit of the Lord God is upon me, because the Lord hath anointed me to preach good tidings unto the meek; he hath sent me to bind up the brokenhearted, to proclaim liberty to the captives, and the opening of the prison to them that are bound.*

I wondered what it all meant. I didn't know for sure. Somebody in that passage was being anointed by God. I guessed that was like having a door opened for you. Whoever was being anointed was meant to do something important with their life. They was destined to do something that mattered, in this case to help folks who was feeling poorly, to help set folks free from the prisons they was in. I wondered who could be a person like that.

Truly, we was all wanting to be set free. Greil was never meant to be a long-term hospital. Its official description was an acute care facility. That meant they was trying to fix you up soon and send you on your way. It wasn't a cruel intention—things weren't like that at a good place like Greil. The purpose of acute care was to get you over a crisis then get you back to your living. They said the average stay at Greil was two months. After that, they was hoping you got better and that you left.

Roshanda was the first person I knowed who left Greil. It was maybe five weeks into my stay. The morning she left she was informing everybody in range about Dorothea Dix, an American activist who created the first modern generation of mental asylums in the late 1800s. Things had gone downhill since Missus Dix's day, Roshanda was shouting. Real bad. But now things were coming back again, they were—it was a new revolution! Roshanda hugged me tight on the way out the door and I hugged her tight back. I had come to like Roshanda just fine.

The queen wasn't too far behind. She left a few days later. Her son and his pretty wife came to get her. The son was dressed in a smart suit and speaking softly to his mother, carrying her suitcase, holding her hand as his wife helped her into their car. I felt sad when my two friends left, but I was happy for them, too. Something was proving hopeful for them. They had places to go. They surely did.

Turns out I didn't need to feel sad very long. Within a week Roshanda was back at Greil. Three days later the queen was back, too. I learned it's pretty common to cycle back in. Life proves hard on the outside.

That first evening when they was both back I joined Roshanda and the queen sitting on the couch in the activity room. The queen was wearing her same old favorite Christmas robe. Roshanda was loud-talking about good times ahead. I didn't doubt that. I really didn't. I didn't doubt that the mental health care system fixed some folks. It wasn't the enemy. Far from it. It was trying as hard as it could to fix us, and it was using all the resources it had available. I was thankful for the mental health care system and its fixing ways. Mighty thankful. But there was a truth of limits I think we were all confronting the longer we was all inside the system: there's only so much help meds and counseling can offer. You need something beyond that if you're gonna truly succeed. I think everybody who stayed at Greil for any amount of time came to know that.

Roshanda's hair had returned to kinky toward the end of her first stay, but she had got it freshened when she had been on the outside because it fell in stylish waves below her shoulders the day she returned. The new look didn't last long. Once more, sitting back on the couch with the queen and me, Roshanda's hair was standing straight up.

The queen wore a curious expression on her fine elderly face that first evening when we was all together. She kept looking at me out of the corners of her eyes. Then she left the couch and shuffled over to a chair about five feet away from me, glancing at me quickly every so often so as not to meet my eye. It must have been a full ten minutes of looking my way before she said, "I have friends here, you know. There's a pretty puzzle too. It shows water lilies when you put it all together." She said this all with a low voice, talking to me as if I was someone she had never met before, beginning to twirl her fingers in her regal hair.

II

The Start of
Being Free

"YOU AIN'T SICK, MARTHA," ROSHANDA said. She was sitting on a chair in the activity room and I was standing behind her with a hairbrush. "How come you even in here?"

I paused, then continued brushing her long, cocoa hair. "I needed to help me," I said. "Nothing was no good, so I had to do something about myself."

The queen was on a couch a few feet away, watching us. She clutched a silver-blue comb in her hands, a little gift that I'd brought her last weekend when I was home. I'd do her hair after Roshanda's. Doing hair was a morning routine we had begun about two months into my stay at Greil. Two months was the mark where I should've been heading back out into the community, but I had decided I wasn't leaving just yet. I'd go home on weekends, sure, to see my boys and Mama and Daddy, but I liked it better here inside the mental hospital. I wasn't exactly sure when I was gonna leave, but so far no administrators were kicking me out, so I was staying. The longer I was here, I was feeling better and better. I wasn't sure if I ever wanted to leave. There was a safety at Greil that I wasn't feeling on the outside.

"What do you keep writing in that notebook of yours, anyway?" Roshanda asked. "You're always scribbling something. Reading that Bible of yours and writing notes—that's all you ever do these days, girl."

"It ain't nothing," I said. "Just letters, mostly."

"Letters to who?" Roshanda said, then remembered her college ways. "I mean to *whom*". She stressed the word coolly. "You keeping a boyfriend hid in your room?"

"Nah, nothing like that." I smiled. I had been doing a lot more of that lately—smiling. "It's hard to explain."

The Match Game came on TV, and Roshanda shushed me because she always watched that. I finished her hair and started in on the queen's. Then I went down to the nurses' station to see if they needed any help. I lent a hand there for a spell, cleaning up, sweeping, just doing whatever I could to be useful. Then they said they was all right for the rest of the morning, so for an hour or so after that I went from room to room visiting folks, asking how they were, seeing if they needed a glass of water or maybe just someone to talk to for a spell. Lots of folks took me up on the offer. That's how my days were going at Greil now. Every morning I made my rounds, doing hair, helping out wherever I could. It felt good to be doing something purposeful. It felt good to be needed.

A job with a purpose goes a long way toward healing a body. That's what I was feeling here. My other job, my money job at Brockway, was still intact during my hospital stay and I was collecting disability, which was keeping the mortgage on my house paid. But as good as that job at Brockway was, I felt a twinge in my spine every time I thought of it. Brockway was a fine company indeed, they paid more than any job I ever knowed, and they was constantly gracious with giving me time off to be sick. But when I was being honest I knowed I dreaded working there. The job at Brockway wasn't me. Standing all day or night beside an assembly line. When I imagined the next thirty-five years doing that I quaked inside. As humble as it was, doing rounds at a mental hospital was doing something on the inside of me that Brockway never could. If I could just keep going at Greil for a spell, getting up every morning, sweeping up, fixing Roshanda's and the queen's hair, helping the nurses out, reading my Bible, writing letters, taking my meds, talking to folks who didn't mind hearing me talk. That was the season of purpose I needed in order to do some healing.

After my rounds I had lunch, a tuna melt and a glass of milk, and then went back to my room to do some reading. Often I was drawn back to the Old Testament. I kept reading and reading, sometimes just in spare moments, sometimes for hours at a stretch. All the characters I was reading about took on new life for me: Moses. Esther. Abraham. Deborah. King David. Solomon. And the verses from Isaiah 61 kept coming back to me. Every time I opened the Bible it kept falling to that page—the words about wounded folks getting healing and folks in prison getting freed. It was almost uncanny.

That's what I was writing about in my notebook all the time. Something new was happening inside of me and I was trying to take in all in. My soul was getting purged and healed from a heap of wounding, and though I still felt shaky I had something solid at last to cling to. Day after day, that solid thing was proving to be God's word. Sure, the meds and counseling was doing something to help too, but the best flood of healing I was drinking in was coming straight from the pages of that old Bible. That's how I was getting through one day to the next—by reminding myself of God's promises every morning, every afternoon, every evening, just reading, reading, reading. That's how I knew that things was gonna be all right someday.

Through the help of one of the counselors at Greil I came to realize that for too many years my true self had been pushed down and silenced by my fearful self. I knew it was time to end that pattern because I didn't want fear holding me back no more. During one of my weekends home from Greil I called a family meeting. All my sisters and brothers came, along with Mama and Daddy. This was something I needed to do: to start telling them the truth.

In a quiet voice I explained that I couldn't make it on the outside unless I knew for sure that I had their support. I knowed they all loved me, but maybe I was just making sure that they heard that cry straight from my lips. In a large family it's easy to not be heard, and I needed to take responsibility for making myself heard, 'cause they didn't know how I felt otherwise. How could they have?

Mama didn't quite understand the meeting's purpose at first. She had been caring for me so strongly and I knowed she was bleeding inside for what I was going through. I tried to explain that I wasn't mad at nobody, particularly Mama. It's just that so much of the time growing up I was trying to be happy on the outside, smiling, supporting what everybody else was thinking, while inside I was dying, screaming, saying help me help me help me. How could they know that unless I told them?

In my depression I used to withdraw from folks, even folks I loved, keeping it all dreary in my house for days on end with the shades drawn. None of my family knew the bulk of that because I wasn't telling them. I hadn't been asking them for the support I needed, and I hadn't been telling them what was truly going on inside of me. That was about the worst kind of deception I could ever have with the folks I loved the most—not telling the truth about me. But I was changing. That's what the conversation with my family was about.

"See, the problem is that you ain't taking responsibility for yourself," Roshanda said as I was fixing her hair. She was having a coherent day with her words, and I was telling her about the meeting I had called with my family. It had seemed to go well. "I don't mean here at Greil, but out there in general. You're a smart woman, Martha. I knowed that the first time I set eyes on you. You might not have schooling, but you could be going places. You still got your dreams. I know you do because you're still living like you got a purpose. You could be doing a lot more with your life. But instead you're in here."

She said the last words with a high-pitched preacher's voice. I paused the brush midstroke and tried to collect my thoughts.

"Oh, you're probably thinking that someone else is to blame for all your problems, but who gives a rip about all them other folks?" Roshanda said. "You're the one who's got to stand up and be counted, Martha. Nobody's gonna hand you happiness on a platter. You got to go out and feel it for yourself."

I finished brushing Roshanda's hair, then spoke quietly. "You don't know all what's happened to me, Roshanda. I got some mighty hard times in my past that I'm trying hard to forget." I was aiming to tell the truth.

"Well boo hoo!" Roshanda said in a rush. "Don't everybody? We all got problems. Don't be letting all those mighty hard times in your past hold you back. What about all the Bible folks you're always reading about? Yeah. I went to Sunday school once too, you know. Adam and Eve was kicked out of Eden. Abraham took a knife to his son. Jonah was ate up by a whale. Did you ever hear them moaning about their troubles? All folks got troubles. But you got to keep going forward, girl. You got dreams to live. You could go to college one day. Or you could own your business, maybe your own hair salon! You could be doing real good things with your life, Martha. Real good things. But instead you're in here."

She repeated that last line as if on intention. That was the end of the hair brushing for the day. Roshanda was making sense, maybe too much sense, but I wasn't summoning the strength to do much forward going just yet. Deep within me I couldn't recall if I had dreams still or not. All I wanted to do was be home fixing supper for my boys. I could envision them sitting around our supper table and me bringing them a big plate of fried chicken with all the collards they could eat. And for dessert there'd be banana pudding. Big bowls all around. And the heavenly smell of that supper would waft all around our kitchen and they'd be laughing and joking and I'd be caring for them, and they wouldn't need to be worried about their mama no more. I just wanted to be a good mama to my boys. If I could just do that, that was dream enough for now.

I walked to my room and pulled out my notebook and a pen. Lately I had taken to writing out my praying. That's what was in all the letters I was writing. I figured God could do all the sorting out of my mind that needed to be done.

Dear God,

I knowed that in the past I been through a heap of trouble, but maybe I can put all them sorrows behind me. I'm aiming to believe you when you say you care for me. So maybe with your help I could do some better things with my life. Maybe I could go back to my boys and be the mama they need. Please help me go back to my boys, God. Just that for now. Will you please help me?

Love, Martha

I went to sleep that night with a settling sense of peace. Next morning I got up, showered, dressed, then caught a glimpse of myself in the mirror. I'd been able to do that for a while now—look at myself in the mirror. At first it had scared me, but my eyes weren't looking as empty now as they had been. This day my hair was smoothed back and my dress was pressed and clean. I even had on a bit of makeup. I wasn't looking like a crazy woman no more. I stood for a moment, just staring at my reflection. There were words I was longing to hear. I decided to say them out loud for myself. I spoke them slowly, taking in the full meaning of each phrase: "Martha, you're okay. You know that? You're really all right, girl."

Those were my words. Sure, I was talking to myself, but it wasn't crazy talk. Crazy talk was calling myself stupid and ugly all the time. I figured I needed to change the way I talked about myself. Yes, I had made my share of mistakes. Some troubles I had made for myself. Others were made to me. But the mistakes were in the past, I couldn't go back and change things. I couldn't go back in time and not be raped. I couldn't push no clock back and make better choices about fellas. I couldn't go back and not be pregnant at fifteen. All I could do is put those things somewhere outside of me and let them go, like a balloon rising in the air, then keep going forward. I knowed God would make all things right someday. God was all about a good kind of justice, if not now, then in the age to come. Martin Luther King Jr. had spoke about it. Justice was gonna roll down like water one day, and righteousness like a mighty stream. Mister King had surely glimpsed that good justice from afar. Now in heaven he was standing next to Jesus and seeing the goodness of God up close. God was gonna set all things right one day. That's how I could let go of my trouble.

Three months after arriving at Greil I collected my notebooks and journals, packed my suitcase, and signed myself out of the hospital. In the entryway I glanced down at that same green-and-white tile floor that had caught and held my eyes so tight ninety days earlier. I looked at the floor. Then I looked ahead.

Roshanda and the queen came to the entryway to see me goodbye. The queen hugged me for a long while. Then it was Roshanda's turn. Tears were coming up in her eyes. They was coming up in my eyes too, but they weren't bad tears. I knew that I could stop them by and by, so I let them fall without regret.

"Don't you ever come back here, Martha," Roshanda whispered in my ear. She was hugging me tight. "You're gonna do something more than this. I knowed it for sure." She gave me another big squeeze and must have thought for a moment 'cause she said, "You only come back to do my hair, you hear?!"

I smiled big and Roshanda laughed through tears. "Well, it's a deal, then," I said. "You keep that brush handy, girl."

A car was waiting. I hugged the doctors and nurses who had made Greil come to feel so much like home for me. Then I walked out the front door. It's true, I wasn't sure that I might not return to Greil. Most folks did return at least a few times, and I wasn't too proud to say that might be me. But I wanted to make it strong on the outside. I wanted to be cooking supper again for my boys. I wanted to see if this new honesty I was feeling would help me express the things inside of me that needed to be talked about. I wasn't pressing my feelings down tight within me no more. The words from the Bible that I kept reading were giving me a new power to try things I would never have thought about trying before. Leaving Greil was one of the first steps.

My resolve was put to a quick test. As soon as I got home to Sheridan Heights, one of my neighbors saw me getting out of the car. She came over, her mouth flapping. "Girl, where you been?" she asked. "I ain't seen you in ages."

"I been staying at Greil," I said.

"Oooh, you shouldn't tell nobody that." Her brow wrinkled and she shook her head.

I thought for a moment, standing outside in my driveway, suitcase in my hand. What was I supposed to say? That I had been away drinking pink lemonade in Maui? That wasn't the truth. And I was only gonna tell the truth. Sure, it was easy to feel disgrace about being in a psychiatric hospital, even about needing help for your emotions. But why did it need to be that way? If I always told the truth then I had nothing to hide. Plenty of folks needed help with something. To get help didn't mean you were weak. Like somebody had to have more sense than you about fixing your car. Or about helping you with your taxes. Nobody did that by themselves. So why should I be thinking I can handle all those heavy emotions by myself? I smiled at my neighbor and looked her in the eye. "It was an okay time at Greil," I said. Then I went inside my house. I wasn't gonna be ashamed of where I'd been. I know I needed help. And help was given me.

Being in my own house again felt good. Real good. My boys were at school but they'd be home again soon and I couldn't wait to say hello and give them all big hugs. Mama had fixed a vase of violets on the kitchen table for me. She had prepared some chicken and dumplings for us to eat the first night. There'd be more help if I needed it, she said. She'd be looking in on me every day for a while. And I was going to be meeting with a counselor for a while as well, just to make sure things were keeping on an even keel. I had a lot of fears still, but I was starting to feel free.

I set my suitcase in my bedroom, wandered out to my living room, and picked up the family Bible from where it sat on a shelf. This wasn't the same old Bible from the activity room at Greil. This was the one I used on Friday night with the boys. Out of habit, I guess, I set the Bible on the coffee table and let it fall open to any old page.

What I have to tell you right now is no lie. It's not something anyone made up for this book so my story would sound better than it really was. And it certainly ain't something I can explain by no natural means. My family Bible wasn't creased in any familiar spots like the Bible at Greil might have been, and my family Bible fell open completely by chance.

That afternoon, coming home from Greil, it opened straight to Isaiah 61. And I took in those same exact few verses that had been so rich to me this past season of my life: *The Spirit of the Lord God is upon me; because the Lord hath anointed me to preach good tidings unto the meek; he hath sent me to bind up the brokenhearted, to proclaim liberty to the captives, and the opening of the prison to them that are bound.*

I still didn't know what it all meant. Somebody in that passage was having a door being opened for them. They was meant to do something important with their life. They was destined to do something that mattered, in this case to help folks who was feeling poorly, to help set folks free. I wondered who could ever be a person like that.

12

A Few Steps Forward

WHEN I HEARD A VOICE in my head this time, I knowed it was different.

To begin with, this voice wasn't trying to be all charming or cunning, and it certainly wasn't trying to persuade me of nothing harmful like taking too many pills or ending my life. This voice wasn't nothing that put fear or doubt or frustration in my head, things to make me feel bad about myself. This voice had a sweet aroma, and it came steaming up to me from the sauce pot of Scripture that I kept reading and reading. This voice felt clean and empowering, and it was talking to me in my own words, and it kept saying things like, "Martha, you're all right, you know that, girl. You really are all right!" I liked how this voice was sounding, this voice of love. I truly did.

"Hey Martha," said the love one day. "I've got a promise for you. Your life is gonna be greater and wilder than you could ever dream. In fact, you wouldn't believe me at first if I told you how good your life is gonna be. So I'm gonna bring you along bit by bit, if you're willing. It'll mean some trusting for you, and I know trusting is hard because you've been hurt before when it comes to trusting. But I'm gonna be there for you always—I'm your security and rock. And good things are ahead, Martha, mighty good things. Keep in mind that all things are possible for those who believe."

Maybe it wasn't all those words. Maybe that's just how I interpret that conversation years later. We was praying, this voice of love and me. I was saying things up to heaven and this love was speaking down. The phrase I remember hearing most clearly during that particular praying time nearly shook me off the commode. I remember it word for word. The phrase was: "Martha, you are destined for greatness." You see, I was praying in my bathroom when I heard that, as funny as it sounds. There was no dominoes in my head this time and no bag of pills under the counter begging for my attention. Maybe the love chose to speak to me in the bathroom to upturn the harm that had been spoken to me in this room before. I don't rightly know. Or maybe, like Jesus got baptized by his cousin John in the muddy Jordan River, the love simply wanted to choose a humble place to start opening doors of opportunity.

Well, I flushed, washed my hands, and said in disbelief, "Me? Greatness? No, God, I don't think so." I couldn't fathom how that could ever come about. There certainly wasn't no heavens parting in my life. No Holy Spirit dove descending on my shoulder. In fact, I wasn't doing nothing impressive in my life at all that I could think of. I didn't have no great dreams like Martin Luther King once talked about. I was just back sweating out my shifts at the glass factory. And I was back at Greil, too—only this time I wasn't staying overnight. I was keeping my agreement to Roshanda and doing her hair and the queen's, coming and going each week to say hello and see if they was okay or needed anything. And I was back making supper for my boys. That was all the greatness I had been dreaming of for some time.

I was truly enjoying my return to my kitchen. I must digress and flap about that for a spell. For if you enjoy cooking and you've been out of your kitchen for a time, and then you get a chance to go back in—*my my my*, the bounties you're gonna whip up. Can you relate? The cooking was flowing out of me as free and easy as breathing. Come the end of every shift at Brockway I was back home clanging spoons and clattering dishes and fixing up meat loaf and fried pork steak and barbecued pork and fried chicken and fried catfish and hollering in a high voice for my boys to come and get it. They was grinning and digging in and shoveling up and I was serving sides of collards and steamed rice and squash casserole and fried green tomatoes, and for dessert they was munching down apple cobbler and raisin bread pudding and chocolate cake and strawberry pie. My boys were patting their tummies and asking for seconds and letting out satisfied sounds of chewing delight at every meal.

There was more celebrating to be done. Soon in those early days after coming back from Greil a holiday came and went—Thanksgiving, it was—and everybody I knowed came over to my house, and I simply went to town. Martha Hawkins was in her right mind and back in her kitchen, she was, and when Martha Hawkins does Thanksgiving, whoo whee, it ain't nothing but a spread. Well, I fixed up a big ole braised roast beef and a tender baked turkey with dressing and gravy and cranberry sauce and mashed potatoes and collards and peas and yams and buttered carrots and potato soufflé. Mmmm mmmph! Let me tell you about that gravy I was making. It was simmering hot on the stove with the finest turkey pieces bobbing all about—'twas the giblets where all the flavor stays—and that gravy, I swear it was so full of joy at the thought of being poured over that meal it was grinning right along with all my family members seated around my table; that gravy just splashed and laughed its way over peas and dressing and white meat and mashed potatoes. And the butter—it came to the dinner with a smiley personality, too. That good country butter was cooked into that feast with all joy I could beckon. It was melting into rolls and caressing those sauces and hugging the carrots and making everybody feel downright giddy. Have you ever felt giddy about butter? Not many folks realize that butter is an intoxicant. When it's made with love it's transformed along the same lines as that miracle wine Jesus dished up at the wedding in Cana. Butter refreshes the heart and soothes the soul and bursts forth from old wineskins because you can't contain the blessed spirit of good country butter. Then for dessert we ate homemade pecan pie and chocolate cake. Then we sat around in my living room and all talked at once. For that's what we do. And if you ever come over to our house today, that's what it's still like. That was our Thanksgiving and we was truly celebrating, we was.

Back to that unlikely phrase I heard in my bathroom, the one that said I was destined for greatness. When I got to pondering that phrase, it set me to scratching my head. There wasn't much greatness where I worked. I must confess I was struggling at Brockway like I had never struggled before. My body was feeling all right, my mind was clear, and I was getting my job done, but I was feeling a sense of dread in my soul that I couldn't shake. The factory work wasn't beneath me—it wasn't nothing like that. But can you recognize dread? It's that thick, dull feeling that there's something more truthful to who you are that you should be doing, but you ain't. That feeling was growing to be an every-shift occurrence. The dread was sticking to my soul like a rotten potato once stuck to the top of my fridge. That potato had rolled back to be unseen and forgotten, and after some time it smelled like a skunk in the dust. That dreadful potato left drippy stuff all over the top of my fridge when I cleaned it up, and that sort of thing never happens in my clean kitchen.

I knowed that part of the dread I was feeling was circulating in from my boys. I wanted to be home with them so I could be the mama they needed. That was the dream of mine. They had spent so much time away from their mama and they were getting bigger now: by 1979 when I was thirty-two and had been out of Greil for about two years Shawn was sixteen; Quintin, thirteen; Reginald, twelve; and Nyrone, ten. They was all doing well in school, studying hard and getting good grades, staying out of trouble and keeping off drugs. Shawn was wrestling and his team took state. Quint and Reginald were playing football and doing real well. Nyrone had a good arm and I knowed he'd be out shining on the field soon. I was so proud of my boys. So proud. But no matter how old a boy gets, he wants his mama to be around while he's still at home. I'm not talking around like she has to be in his business every moment. But at those moments when a boy needs her, he wants her to be around. I can't explain that longing of a child by any better word than "around."

Driving home from a shift at Brockway early one morning in my old brown Pinto, I had the radio on, it was that Bible teacher Charles Stanley from the First Baptist Church of Atlanta. Now, I ain't trying to press a particular preacher on you because you may have different beliefs than Reverend Stanley, but what he was preaching that day was making a heap of sense to me. He was preaching that the good Lord can do a mighty work both in you and through you if you just step out on his promises. Why, the circumstances in front of you may seem unclear, the Reverend Stanley was saying, and if God wants to open a door of opportunity for you he may need to close one too. You may need to end a friendship that's pulling you in a harmful direction, or move away from a neighborhood that's causing you distress, or you may even need to quit a job . . .

The radio crackled and I wasn't listening no more. Reverend Stanley's voice soon came back on clear and flowing, but I couldn't listen. I was crying. I hadn't been crying hardly at all no more. But this was a different cry. I was crying because I knew what I needed to do. A big and good door was opening for me and I needed to walk through it in order to step into God's promise. Yet I was scared.

Mighty scared. I had bills to pay. Boys to feed. A mortgage every month. I couldn't be doing what I know I needed to do.

"Martha," said the love as we approached my driveway. "You don't need to worry, girl—I'm gonna supply all you need according to my riches." I think I had read that in the Bible somewhere. Walking up to my front door I saw that my boys were all home. Shawn could look after things just fine when I was at shift now. Still, it was a fresh realization that they had been at home alone, and I hadn't been around.

My pay at Brockway had been raised to $14 an hour. Thankfully, over the last bit of time I had managed to pay off the bills from my medical co-pays and whatnot from Greil and the surgeries; I had even stored up a bit of a nest egg. But all that wasn't gonna last long, and no other moneymaking plans were coming to mind other than stepping forward. For a good three days I wavered, not sure that my stepping could be firm.

On the third day I was reading in the Old Testament about how Abraham was called to leave his country and all he knew and head for a new land. That was Abraham's invitation of faith: to step surely. That was my answer. The words burst off the page toward me. My life without God hadn't been working—I had already tried that. But my new life with God was working, so I was gonna do whatever God said, no matter what it was.

I quit my job. I just stepped forward and quit.

The boys loved it. For once I was truly around. And I loved it too. It was so much simpler to keep my mind at ease. It's hard to fully explain how hard it had been to be a single working mother of four boys for all those years beforehand, even when they were good boys. But when you've got a full-time job and you're a full-time mama, there ain't no rest in a situation like that. Ever. You're always worrying about this or that—and you're doing all your worrying by yourself. Now I had nothing left except God. I was letting go and going in his direction. That's all I knew to do.

A month went by.

Another month.

Three months.

Then the bulk of our savings was used up.

We needed to have some finances coming in. I was praying and praying but not getting no clear answer. A friend suggested public assistance. You heard a lot about that in the projects where plenty of folks was on public assistance. It didn't seem entirely right to do, but I remembered what Daddy had said. Some things the government did were designed to give folks a hand up. It was okay to accept help if the hand helped you go forward, but if the hand that helped you kept you stuck then it wasn't no use and you wasn't to take it. Well, I was going forward. It wasn't no easy decision, that's for sure. I was proud that I had always worked even though I was a single mother. Mighty proud. This sure didn't seem like no path to greatness that God would choose for me. For several days I let the decision roll around in my mind.

One morning my answer came to me quietly. As much as I thought I was already humble, the fact was that I was feeling too uppity to go on public assistance. It was pride that was keeping me back, ugly pride, plain and simple. Not the good kind of pride that says go out and get a job—I already had that. This was a pride telling me I was better than folks. That uppitiness was keeping me stuck in harmful ways. Step low, Martha, the voice of love was saying, so that the greatness that comes to your life isn't summoned from inside of you. You're more capable than you know, and when the season of greatness comes, I don't want you ever taking credit that you climbed up there by yourself. So step low and humble yourself, and God will lift you up in due time.

Not everybody has understood the decision. They didn't then, and they don't today.

"Welfare?" Roshanda shouted. I was back at Greil one morning doing her hair. "You quit your job at Brockway and went on welfare? What were you thinking, girl? You're crazy! Plumb crazy! You need to come back inside here to Greil because you done lost your mind!"

"I can't quite rightly explain it myself," I said. "All I know is this is something God wants me to do."

"That don't seem like no God I know, Martha. Where's the cattle on a thousand hills that he's always bragging about? If I was God, you know what I'd do? Martha Hawkins would win the lottery and she'd be rich!"

"I know what you mean, Roshanda." I sighed and shook my head. "If I was God, I'd have me win the lottery, too."

Public assistance, for all the fuss made about it, wasn't much. It meant food stamps to keep us eating, health care for the kids and me, which a mother is mighty grateful for, and a grand total of $177 per month. My mortgage was $322 alone. Folks on welfare weren't meant to live in no suburban houses—that's what welfare was telling me, anyway.

I should let you in on this decision, too, while I'm thinking about it. About this time I started doing something else I never figured on. You can rail against me all you want, but it don't matter now. I figured if I was stepping out on faith then I was gonna step all the way, so I started giving money away. It was hilarious if you think about it: me, on welfare, giving money to other folks. There's a story about Jesus praising an old widow who put her last two pennies into the temple treasury and I imagined myself following her example. I figured even if I had only two pennies to give, maybe there's folks out there who only have one penny, or no pennies at all. So on habit I started giving away $20 a month, about 10 percent of what I was bringing in. I heard that God loves it when we become givers. It's our character he likes to shape. When we become givers, particularly if we stretch our limits, the blessing comes back to us and it's always ours to keep. So I was gonna become a giver, even though more than one person I knowed flat out called me crazy.

Public assistance allowed you to make a little money, too, as long as you didn't go over a threshold. I figured I could work part-time and bring in some extra cash to keep the mortgage alive. What else did I know how to do except cook? Back at Brockway I had baked cakes and pies for folks at Christmas, so I decided to keep going that direction and went around to businesses and factories and started a lunch service. I typed up menus, then took orders—the menu changed every day—fried fish, chicken sandwiches, hot apple pie, peach cobbler for dessert. Folks called me before 10 o'clock to place an order. Then I cooked up the orders and delivered the food around at lunchtime. One person at each business collected the money for me and I gave them a free lunch in exchange. Pretty soon I had a regular rotation of two different businesses each day of the workweek. I delivered the lunches in my Pinto.

Along with this, every Saturday I set out an impromptu all-you-can-eat buffet at my house. Four dollars bought you a full stomach. Word got around and folks came by, friends, family, neighbors; I cooked and they piled their plates. About fifteen to twenty folks were coming regularly before long. The money coming in wasn't making nobody rich—we was even going down a bit every month as expenses kept going up and I wasn't raising prices—but I was managing to keep the mortgage paid and the lights on. That was my main goal just then—keeping a good roof over my boys' heads so we didn't have to go back to the projects.

This dabbling in the cooking business started me remembering that dream I had when I was a child. I had forgotten it in the years since. That dream came after Edward and I had got lost at Trenholm Court and we had found our way home again. I was sitting at the table eating that salty and smooth pork chop casserole with my mama and daddy and all my brothers and sisters, and I dreamed of opening a restaurant someday that felt just like that, a place that when people was out getting lost and doing whatever people do to feel tight inside that they could come into my restaurant and feel like they had come home. It was still a dream now, although it had been buried for so many years I had near forgot it. Every once in a while, when no one was looking, I'd drive around town, or search the want ads for buildings that were renting out, thinking that maybe I could get my own restaurant someday. In quiet times with the Lord I could see that restaurant in my mind shimmering like a vision. But when I was out driving, looking, rent was always out of reach.

In the spring of 1981, a glorious day came and went. That was the day when my first baby, Shawn, graduated from high school. We held a big party with lots of food, and all the family came over. My boys were doing me so proud. And not only that, but Shawn got scholarships and a Pell Grant, and he was going to college! College! Mmmmm mmmph! Did you ever think a word could sound as pretty as that? Late that summer we went to a yard sale and I bought Shawn two used suitcases before he left home. I wished I had the cash to buy him some new clothes or something. Shawn had $300 in his pocket from money he saved, and to get to school he hitched a ride with a neighbor who was heading over yonder in the same direction. Shawn entered the University of Alabama at Birmingham and started work on a degree in criminal justice. All those years of being the man of the house had honed his aptitude for sensing right and wrong. He wrote a letter soon to say he had found work in the university library, so he was able to make enough money to keep going. I sent letters to him, lots of letters, just saying how proud of him I was, and whenever I could I cooked up a big dinner—enough for him and all his friends to enjoy—and found a way to take it up to the university. The good smells of those dinners would float down the hallway of the dorm, and all his friends came running. That was a good time, such a good time, though it was a painful time too. I wish I could have done more for my son.

About that time my other three boys were afforded a blessing as well. Public schools were getting rougher. More drugs, gangs, and fighting. I sure didn't want my boys to get messed up in that. We was going to an Assemblies of God church then and they had a private school on campus with real good teachers, sports, and academic programs. I wanted my boys to go to that private school. Real bad. It cost big money to get in and I didn't have nothing close to that. So I started praying, God, just let these boys go to school here, please, please, please. Every Sunday I sat in the sanctuary during services, not listening to the preacher like I was supposed to, just praying that my boys could go here to school.

Seems like the Lord was working in the boys' minds, too, because they hatched a plan that started the ball rolling. The school had good basketball and football teams, and the boys were good at both, so they decided to try out for the school's football team. They wasn't enrolled at the school or nothing. I don't rightly know how all that works, but anyway they made the team no problem. Sure enough, we got a phone call one day.

"Martha Hawkins?"

"Yes."

"This is the principal of the Bell Rose Christian School. How'd you like your boys to attend here this fall?"

"Well, that sounds mighty good. But I don't know how that gonna happen except by a miracle."

"Miz Hawkins, we're prepared to offer your boys sports scholarships to attend this school. Full rides. We'll send the paperwork to you in the mail. What do you say?"

"Full rides?"

"Yes Ma'am. You don't need to pay for a thing."

When I hung up the phone I whooped and hollered and raised a happy ruckus till I was wore out from it. The boys whooped and hollered too. I was so thankful to the school for those scholarships that I helped out there by cleaning up the place on weekends. I learned to drive their bus and helped pick people up for Sunday services. I felt indebted to the school, so I did what I could.

That was a mighty good season, the Lord was working powerfully in so many good ways, but there was still one area I couldn't figure out. Money. It got tighter and tighter. I kept praying and taking part-time jobs, but one bill got behind and then another. Most days I was feeling a tightness in my throat, but the Lord kept telling me to cast all my anxiety on him, so that's what I kept doing.

I don't remember which break in the semester it was, but Shawn came home to surprise us. I guess he was most surprised because he got home and all our lights was off. He knocked on the front door 'cause he didn't have his key with him and Reginald answered. Quint and Nyrone were staying over at Mama's house. Shawn came back to the bedroom where I was lying. For as good as I was feeling, there were still some times when I felt best by lying down. Today was one of these days. Shawn had a candle with him that Reginald had given him.

"What's the matter, Mama? Why are all the lights in the house turned off?"

I couldn't turn to face him. My college boy. He was doing so well. I didn't want to distract his ways.

"Mama," he repeated. "Tell me, what's going on?"

Sitting up, I tried to smile. I wondered if he could tell I'd been crying. "Oh, it's nothing you need to worry about," I said. "We're just going through a rough patch right now. These things happen, you know."

"It's the utilities, isn't it? Mama. Why didn't you tell me? I've got money from my Pell Grant. I could have given you some of that money."

"It's gonna get better," I said. "The Lord is gonna make a way."

"Mama, you and family always come first," Shawn said. His voice was firm. "We're gonna get these lights back on."

The lights did come back on. And Shawn went back to college. God was doing something good in my life. I didn't know exactly what, but he had promised there was greatness to come. So that's what I kept believing.

Somewhere it says that God's path is narrower than we think. All are welcome but fewer find that path than not. I wondered if maybe I was missing it somewhere. Surely I saw this blow heading our way. Maybe I had fought it off as long as I could. What came to us wasn't easy for the authorities to do, I knowed that. At our front door one day stood the sheriff. The mortgage wasn't getting paid. Shoot—I hadn't paid it for months. The money just wasn't there. So the sheriff took off his ten-gallon hat with one hand, and with our eviction notice in the other he smoked a cigar from one corner of his jowly mouth and snuffed the ashes that floated down on his suspenders. He was real polite for the business he was doing—I'm grateful for that—but he was firm too. Our time was up. We needed to go. This had been our home for years, the home I bought with Brockway money that lifted us up out of the projects. It pains you something fierce when you lose your home. I can't tell you the despair I felt, the sadness and fear.

We moved out of Faro, the boys and me, and searched around the city for various places we might afford. On the outskirts of town was an old shotgun house for rent. As I stepped up on the porch, my shoe crashed right through. I wasn't fighting with God no more. "Lord, your ways are not our ways," I said, "and I don't want to live in this old shotgun house, but if you want us living here, we'll do it."

God said to keep going, I think. So we kept searching and finally found a house to rent over on Union Street. It wasn't as bad as the shotgun house but it wasn't great neither. The folks who owned it let me have it at a good price because the grass and trees had grown up and I agreed to fix it up. It was full of unseen holes. During the cold months the wind whipped through those walls and the gas bill proved lofty because you couldn't keep heat inside. Come January it was so drafty I'd cook a meal and set it on the table, and in the time it took from stove to plate, the meal turned cold.

'Round then I found part-time work with two older ladies. They called me Little Sunshine. One was ninety-seven years old and suffered from Alzheimer's. For five hours each day I sat with her and took care of her while my boys were at school. I helped her get dressed and with her meals. Sometimes I bathed her. Sometimes she was sick and I need to clean up for her. Folks can get downright messy when they ain't in their right mind, but I didn't fault the woman. The memory of not being in your right mind was still fresh for me.

We needed to move again. With every prayer sent heavenward I resisted going back to the projects. Time passed and there wasn't no other plans I could muster up. God was being silent. At least the projects kept the wind out. We shivered in the Union Street house for a year, then found a place in Cedar Park, a subsidized housing complex on the other side of town from Trenholm Court. I knew we was just passing through. Maybe a couple years or so at best. That's what I kept telling myself, anyway. There was no other choice.

That first night back in the projects I stood outside on the porch a long time. The boys was inside unpacking their things from boxes. In the distance I heard police sirens. Neighbors were yelling angrily at each other across the way. Lines of laundry blew aimlessly in the night air. With my jaw set I faced heaven. I wasn't keeping that agitation inside, that frustration racing through my soul. I started laying that bristling out on the only person I knowed who was listening. I began praying to the voice of love, to the one I had come to know in that past season of time, and it was furious praying too. God, here I am following you with all I know. Here I am stepping forward on faith. Here I am welcoming your promises into my life. But here I am back in the projects living on welfare. Is this your plan for greatness?

God was listening to my vexation, I was sure, and I knew his character could handle my uproar. For some time, that last thought was my only consolation.

13

The Places
You'll Go

IT STARTED RAINING THAT NIGHT in the projects, a real downpour. It hardly ever rains in Montgomery, but just like that rain that kept me out of the eighth-grade homecoming parade, that night it soon got to thundering down with the power of Elijah, and sheet after sheet of lightning bolted across the sky.

There on the porch I listened carefully to the storm above the sound of my wailing to God, but I didn't hear nothing that was making sense. The wind picked up and those lines of laundry started whipping themselves in the dark. All was flap, flap, flapping and gates were banging on their hinges and wadded-up newspaper blew by like tumbleweeds, but still there was no sound that I knew. Then came fire.

I saw it raging across the rooftops on the horizon all orange and red glowing, and heard the fire trucks racing across town to meet that fire of fury, but I still didn't hear nothing I was expecting to hear.

At last there came another noise, and this one was different than all the rest. I was wearing a shawl across my shoulders to keep out the cold, sort of a large scarflike thing, and when I heard the noise it was still and small, so I pulled the scarf about me and went indoors. All my crying and moaning was finished for a spell and I was listening now. I took a look around at our new, low-income apartment. The boys had emptied most of the boxes, ripped them down, and stacked them to be taken to the Dumpster. Dishes and plates were unwrapped and piled in rows in the cupboards. Everything was getting set up and put into place. My favorite chair was right by my lamp where I liked it. The action felt most logical for me to do, so I went over to my chair, sat down on it, and put my head in my hands, straining my ears to hear.

"Martha, can you hear me?" came a voice. It was familiar. Real soft. Real clear.

"Yes," I said. "Please keep speaking."

"Martha, do you know whose daughter you are?"

Now, that was a question I hadn't expected. "Yes, my daddy is Willie Hawkins. He used to ride his bicycle to the fertilizer factory before he retired. Now he cleans the floors at the elementary school."

"He's a good man, isn't he," said the voice.

"Yes. I love him so."

"But, Martha. I'm asking something different. Do you know what I'm asking you here?"

I didn't know how to answer the voice this time. I decided to stay silent. The voice kept on speaking, repeating the same line of questioning. "Martha, I'm asking about your identity. Willie Hawkins is your daddy, but do you know whose daughter you are?"

The voice's tone was rising, not angry-like, and I didn't doubt its familiarity, but try as I might I couldn't rightly discern what it was asking me. Outside, the storm was still raging, wind and rain and fire and sirens were a-blowing and a-thundering. Inside my new apartment in the projects it was quiet and calm, like I was standing in the mouth of a cave.

The voice kept speaking. "Martha, I know you're upset about where you are right now, but did you ever think that maybe, just maybe . . ." The voice stopped and searched, almost like it was hunting for the right words. "Did you ever think that being on welfare and living in the projects might be the exact ingredients you need to mix up a batter of good opportunity?"

I almost laughed. Yes sir, I could picture it: open the oven, shove in the batter, and out pops a dessert of delight. That was a concept I could get my mind around. I flopped open my Bible to the book of Genesis and started reading. The particular story started with Joseph and his coat of many colors. That boy of so much privilege might have been a favored son by his daddy Jacob, but the young Joseph and his uppity ways had a mighty rough go of it from the start. After getting sold into slavery by his very own brothers, he was accused by Potiphar's wife of a crime of passion he didn't commit. Joseph soon found himself staying in Pharaoh's dungeon, sifting through hay with a lot of time on his hands.

"Keep reading," the voice said. "Just keep reading."

Well, it looked to me like Joseph started mixing up the batter of opportunity. He blended his know-how with his responsibilities and put his shoulder into the stirring of the recipe. The warden noticed it and soon put him in charge of all the other prisoners. Then, still in that circumstance of lockdown, Joseph started meeting folks he might not have otherwise met—the king's baker and butler, to name two. Those two men was well connected and both had fitful dreams and needed a man of vision to help them know what to make of it all. Joseph started praying, seeing from a distance the substance of glory from inside those prison walls. He interpreted the dreams all right and one man went up and the other went down. Soon Joseph was released, and with his newfound talent of dream explaining, he went on to become second in command of all of Egypt. He ended up saving his own family from the seven skinny cows of famine that would have surely devoured them all. None of that goodness might have happened unless Joseph had once been placed in jail.

"I want you to take a good look around you, Martha," the voice was saying. "These boxes, these dishes on your counter, this chair, this lamp—this stub of a welfare check and apartment in the projects. These are all part of my path of promise. It doesn't seem like it now, but you'll see for yourself soon enough. Oh—and keep thinking about the question I asked, the one about whose daughter you are. If you don't figure it out shortly, I'll let you know when the time is right."

Just like that I was all alone. My conscience was clear from having railed against God. There was no sin in it, I was sure. The Almighty was simply fielding all the emotions I gave to him and he was surely big enough to handle that. Inside my heart I still wanted to keep taking steps forward, I truly did; the thing that pumped my blood was still willing. I wasn't sure exactly what the Lord wanted me to do right then except walk within the paths of his promise, so until I heard something specific I figured that in the meantime he'd want me to do whatever I could. Quint had set up the rabbit ears on our old TV already, so I flipped the set on. Part of my motivation for going forward would come from that unlikely source.

They was broadcasting late that night. Maybe the storm had slowed things down. Healthcliff Huxtable was wearing his Technicolor sweaters and busy being a doctor, and Clair his wife was happy being a mama and a lawyer at the same time, and little Rudy was busy having a funeral for her pet fish, Lamont. I started to laugh and wiped my eyes. Going to the kitchen I fished out a soda from the icebox then came back and continued watching. The boys were all in bed by then and I was alone in front of the TV. I loved *The Cosby Show* and watched it every Thursday night when I could.

During a commercial they announced some grand news: *The Cosby Show* was the number one TV show in America. Imagine that.

My favorite show was number one. Then came on some interview show saying how some folks were upset about that fact. They was arguing that *The Cosby Show* was telling folks that blacks have only themselves to blame if they don't succeed in society, and that *The Cosby Show* made it sound like the bigger issues of racism that so many folks had been struggling against for so many years didn't amount to a heap of spit.

The news blurb went off and a rerun of *Laverne & Shirley* came on. It was the one where Lenny has "One Wolf" embroidered on the back of his jacket by mistake, then Laverne feels sorry for him and gives him one of her sweater L's and Lenny becomes the "Lone Wolf." I had seen it before and it was a real funny to me but I wasn't laughing now. I was thinking real hard. To me, folks had to know firsthand how difficult the times had been. Shoot, how difficult the times still was. I wasn't mad at *The Cosby Show* at all. No sir. Its success felt like the result of a bigger sort of triumph to me. I was happy the show was number one. Did folks catch the significance of what that meant? Some larger dreams of equality and opportunity were being played out right before our eyes. *The Cosby Show*—and all it stood for—actors and TV shows and athletes and folks of prominence doing good things like that young Oprah Winfrey and that Pulitzer Prize–winning Alice Walker whose book I had just read—they was all a testament to the quiet force of the movement's continued progress.

Simply by himself, Dr. Bill Cosby was a one-man testament to that quiet force of progress. A few days later I picked up a magazine in the grocery store and thumbed through an article about him that said his mama was a maid and his daddy was a cook in the navy. Now, those were beginnings I could identify with. Although his start had been lowly, Mister Cosby had gone on to do something great with his life and had been helped mightily along in that direction by education. Maybe that's what I needed: some more of that. Right there in the aisle with the cans of tuna and Hamburger Helper I prayed and it sounded like the Lord was saying yes. I could certainly use more education than I had; anytime I filled out a job application, my lack of a diploma made me wince. It took a while to get everything in order, but that day a new plan was set.

In 1985 when I was thirty-eight I signed up and made it official. The opportunities of higher education had become part of my family's ways, and I knew I wanted to be a part of those ways, too. Quint had already graduated high school and gone on to Auburn University for a degree in business administration. Reginald was going to graduate high school soon and go to Tennessee State University to study mass communication. Nyrone had a few years of high school left but was doing real fine and eyeing Memphis State with a nod to getting a degree in communications and cultural diversity. They was being an example to me, and I hoped I was being an example to them by continuing on as well.

So I went over to Alabama State University and signed up to take my GED test. Fear had kept me from doing that for so many years, but it wasn't that hard when I put my mind to it. I took a class first and got some books and studied every night for some time and passed the test the first time around. I felt good about that, real good, passing that GED on my first try.

Next thing you know, I was enrolling in college. Troy State University was just down the street from me so I started taking classes in sociology, English, and psychology. I figured that with all I had been through I should become a counselor. The idea of helping folks sounded good to me so I aimed for a certification. The studying came easier to me than I first thought it would. I discovered I knew how the mind worked and I wanted to help people, so the coursework proved a natural fit.

Time went on and things were going well at university, but the more studying I did, I got to thinking that being a counselor maybe wouldn't be the best fit for me after all. Sitting in a chair all day listening to folks wasn't my style. But being up and around and busy, working with stoves and plates and fried chicken and buffets—that was something I always pictured myself doing. Maybe counseling was gonna become part of that dream, fitting in with it in natural ways. I knowed that folks love to talk when they eat, so I figured that folks could come to the restaurant I was gonna own someday and talk and eat at the same time, and then they'd feel better afterward. That was what counseling was aiming to do all along, wasn't it? I don't mean that it was gonna be a restaurant for folks from the loonybin, although they would be welcome if ever they stopped by. It was just gonna be a place of sound talk. Just day-to-day wisdom where folks could learn to know what was real. With this in mind, I started stepping forward even more, putting pots and pans away on layaway, praying and dreaming of the day when my restaurant would come to be.

Still, that dream felt a long way off, and in the meantime, the last thing I ever wanted to do without a full-time job was have idle hands. Reverend King was never just a dreamer; he was a doer, too. Caring for my boys took a lot of my time, true, but I figured I could do something more than I was doing in addition to that.

My church had a volunteer group called the Matrons who were always on the lookout for new members. They was all kindly senior women with silver hair and gnarled hands, and it seemed that a bunch of younger women all joined the Matrons at once in a rush—me being one—all of us looking for something helpful to do. Somebody from the original group fussed that all the new folks was too much change too soon, then one of the new young folks said, "Hey, I ain't very *matronly* anyway," so all us new folks branched off and started our own group with a new title called the Young Matrons. Being in a new group seemed to suit us fine.

Must have been the same holy fire in our new group because we all got busy right away doing whatever we could think of to help out our communities. We worked with kids and cleaned stuff up and bought new toys and raised money for new educational materials for anybody who needed some freshness in their mind. We drew up a list of shut-ins who needed help cleaning their houses or getting groceries, and we started helping out there. The folks we called on was real happy with that plan. Then we started visiting the women's prison, trying to encourage the folks there who needed some hope. Every other week for some time we went and met with the prisoners and talked with them one-on-one. It was providing some good counseling experience for me, but I wasn't doing it for just that reason. That verse from Isaiah 61 kept burning in my mind, the one about setting captives free. I wasn't about to spring nobody out of jail, but talking with the prisoners felt like an everyday way of living out that verse—to help folks see beyond the cement walls and bars that had locked them in.

Our group really got on a roll, we did, just plowing the hard earth wherever we was able. Our motto was that if you're waiting for somebody else to do something, it will never get done. So we just went. Soon we started a program called the Big A Club for kids from low-income families. We went over to Trenholm Court to play games with them and organized drama classes and hopefully encouraged the children in the projects that someone cared about them. The Big A stood for Attitude, it was all about having a good one, and ten of us ladies from the Young Matrons went over every week to help out. Kids were loving it, and the church must have liked what we were doing, for soon I ended up being elected president of the general mission of the church. I felt good about that role, but it only meant something to me as long as we were doing something good for other folks. That was the real badge of honor.

A company was doing some construction work in Trenholm when we were down there, and I started talking with the folks because I heard they needed some office help. The man in charge offered me a part-time job for about a year in the office doing paperwork. I took the job because the hours were flexible, and I was able to go off public assistance for that time when I was bringing in enough for my boys and me to live on. The job was finished when the construction work was done, then the company moved to Dothan to do another project there. They said I could come over with them and keep working, but I couldn't leave my kids to go that far away. So I went back on public assistance.

Around that time I met a woman named Sophia Bracy Harris who went to the same church as me and was also active in the Young Matrons. She wore her hair in a short Afro and was well dressed and well-spoken, about my age. Sophia spoke with authority and power. Whenever Sophia spoke, people listened. That was mighty impressive to me because I never felt like I had nothing of a voice within me. Sure, I could talk to folks by themselves about important matters, or get up in front of the kids in Trenholm Court and say something, but the thought of speaking in public like Sophia regularly did set my heart to quaking. Those little talks I did in Trenholm were keeping my mind sharp because I had to prepare for a long while beforehand anytime I gave them, but I could never be nothing like Sophia Bracy Harris. The lady was a first-class public speaker who spoke to inspire.

Sophia had helped start another, much larger group called FOCAL (the Federation of Child Care Centers of Alabama) and was now executive director of the group. The purpose of FOCAL was to help out the children of poor folks all across the state of Alabama. Sophia asked me to join the group although I didn't have no kids in child care no more myself. There was a heap of smart and successful women involved with FOCAL from a lot of different cities, including Birmingham, Tuscaloosa, and Huntsville. Sophia and I started going to their conferences in these various cities and meeting people involved with the group, and I soon saw that there was a whole other world out there I didn't know nothing about. I was meeting community leaders, teachers, child care professionals, directors, home providers—basically anybody who had a deep, driving concern for helping kids. Shoot, it seemed everybody I met had so many degrees behind their names they could have given me two or three and never missed a beat. Sophia said the group was all about transforming lives through vision and leadership, which sounded good to me. My figuring was that it seemed a good way to hang out with folks who knew a heap more about life than I did. Some of their smarts was bound to rub off in my direction.

"Say, Martha, what are you going to do with your life, anyway," Sophia asked me one day as we was cleaning up from leading a kids' drama club in Trenholm Court.

"I don't rightly know, Sophia," I said. "Mostly I'm just trying to step into God's promises for my life."

"Yes, and what specifically might that look like?"

"Well . . ." I hesitated, fearing she'd laugh if she heard the specifics of my dream. Sophia knew quite a bit about me by then, where I had come from and what I had been through. She knew I was living in the projects and on welfare—I didn't hide those things from nobody. I decided to blurt out what I hoped for: "I always wanted to own my own restaurant. And not no ordinary restaurant neither. I want to own a special restaurant where folks can eat good food and talk about the things that matter and sort through life and feel good afterward."

Sophia didn't laugh at my mouthful of dreams. She didn't laugh at all. Instead she smiled and said, kinda with a nudge, "So what's holding you back?"

Was she nuts? She knew my story. I decided to play along. "Well, I don't have no money. And I've looked around at commercial sites for years but I've never found a place I could come close to afford to rent. I've only begun to make a dent into my education. And I don't know much about running no business. And—you know this always looks good on a résumé—I was once in a mental hospital. Those are just the starters, I guess."

Sophia squinted. "Martha, you never know what you're capable of until you try. There's real leadership in Alabama! *Real* leadership!" She emphasized the word while looking straight in my eyes. "People from any circumstance can organize themselves, educate themselves, and work together in their communities to make things better. And Martha"—she nodded and raised her eyebrows—"you're one of those leaders."

My eyes flew open wide. I had never thought of myself in those terms. "I don't know about that, Sophia," I said. "I just don't know."

Sophia continued to put away toys and books. She must have been thinking because after a few minutes of silence she said, "Listen, Martha, you like to cook, right? There's a group of women I want you to meet. They've got a weeklong conference coming up and they need someone to do meals for them. You could attend the conference for free and there's a stipend, too. You interested?"

"I guess so." I shrugged. What did I have to lose?

So through Sophia I was introduced to the members of SWEC (Southeast Women's Employment Coalition). The group aimed to help folks in low-income situations make better lives for themselves. They held workshops all over, and meetings each week, and each year they had a six-month-long leadership program. They was a bunch of smart and savvy women.

SWEC must have liked my cooking just fine because I soon made friends all around, and the next thing you know they said I should apply for their leadership program. Well, Sophia's words about leadership and possibility were still ringing in my ears, so I applied and wouldn't you know it, I was accepted. Soon, SWEC was sending me to all these conferences all around the country that aimed to boost my leadership skills and abilities. I had never thought of myself as having any of those, but I guess they thought I did, because next thing you know I was on their board of directors. Soon they've got a leadership conference coming that's going to be all the way up in Washington, D.C., and I'm set to attend. The conference was all about low-income housing. Now, that was something I knowed about.

Seeing Washington felt like another new world to me. The White House. The Lincoln Memorial. The Washington Monument. The Capitol building. The Supreme Court. The Smithsonian. The Library of Congress. All of America's symbols of opportunity seemed to merge in the city and come together as one.

It was summer when I went, and the conference was held on

the campus of Howard University, an institution that had come to play such an important role in American history and the movement. I went to the library and read up on Alain Locke, the first black Rhodes Scholar and father of the Harlem Renaissance, and Ralph Bunche, the first Nobel Peace Prize winner of African descent, both professors at Howard University. Stokely Carmichael, Rayford Logan, E. Franklin Frazier, Sterling Allen Brown—all strong activists in the movement, all connected to the school. Thurgood Marshall had studied at Howard and had later used Howard as the site with his team of legal scholars from around the nation to prepare *Brown v. Board of Education*. Standing on the campus of Howard, looking up into the clear blue sky against the backdrop of Founders Library with its mighty spire and stalwart brick front, it was like the voice of love was telling me that all are equal, all are free, and all deserve the chance to pursue their full measure of happiness.

For several days I just soaked in the sights while attending seminars at the conference. I made a lot of new friends and attended a few board functions and stored all the new experiences within my being. Toward the end of the conference I was strolling across the lawn in front of Founders Library minding my own business when two women I recognized came running toward me at full speed.

"Martha! Martha!" they said. They were fellow board members of SWEC. "We've been looking for you everywhere. You'll never guess what! We've been asked to . . ." The woman doing the last bit of talking needed to pause and take in air.

"The chance of a lifetime!" said the other. "We just held a planning meeting—it was unexpected and we couldn't find you, but they want us to speak! They want us to tell them what things are really like!"

I was smiling and happy for them because they seemed so excited, but I had no idea what they were talking about. "Well, slow down a spell," I said. "What good opportunity? Where?"

"The Capitol!" said the first. "They want us to speak before the United States Senate! Us—the conference leadership! They heard we were over here at Howard and they want us to give a presentation about low-income housing at the Senate! Tomorrow!"

My mouth flew open.

"Not only that, Martha," said the other. Her eyes twinkled. "We held a vote while you were out, and it's you. Martha—we selected you. Who knows more about this subject firsthand? You're going to give the speech tomorrow!"

My jaw dropped to the lawn.

Everything started swelling inside my body as I struggled to make sense of the enormity of what they was saying. My legs went like jelly. My brain felt like a stewpot on fire. My arms flopped like noodles on a kitchen floor. Soon my body caught motion before I could make sense of my tongue and I started shaking my head and backing up. "No no no," I said. "Absolutely no. I could never do that. I don't know nothing about public speaking. What would I ever say?" I thought for a moment and rolled my eyes in utter lostness. "And what would I ever wear?"

"You are our choice, Martha," said the first woman. "You know this stuff. You've been listening at our sessions. Just speak from your heart and tell them what it's really like."

I kept wobbling like a bowl of loose grits. Could this really be something I was meant to do? The U.S. Senate? That was way beyond me, but the women kept nodding their heads so fiercely, all persistent smiles. "Let me go phone my mama," I said. "I'll let you know in an hour."

"Oh Martha!" said Mama over the phone. Her voice was strong, full of pride. "You've come to this place for such a time as this. Trust God. He'll give you the right words to say."

I hung up the phone and dropped to my knees. I was really shaking now.

"Voice of love," I prayed. "This must be your sense of humor 'cause I don't know nothing about public speaking and I've never really done it before 'cept to kids in Trenholm Court. Now you're giving me this chance to speak, my very first chance, and it's to help things change for the better, and that's something I know you want. But this is in front of the United States Senate! Do you remember who I am? This is so far beyond what I can do. But I want to be willing, so I'm inquiring of you. Is this truly something you want me to do?"

Then I listened.

Flipping through my Bible I came to that passage in the Old Testament where God tells Moses to go speak before Pharaoh. The burning bush is all alight and not burning up and Moses has his shoes off because he's standing on holy ground and God is telling him that the slaves in Egypt need to be free. But Moses is afraid. "I don't know nothing about public speaking," Moses says, or words to that effect. But the Lord says, "Who gave man his mouth? Who gives sight or makes him blind? Now go, and I will help you speak and will teach you what to say."

I closed the Bible and the voice of love was speaking to me and there was no silence involved with his words. "I was with Moses, and I'll be with you," God was saying. "Martha, keep stepping forward. This is something I want you to do."

So I said yes.

Oh, that one little word. *Yes.* What a heap of trouble it can bring. All that night I tossed and turned. I worried about everything. I worried about what I was gonna say. I worried about how I would sound. I worried about how I was gonna do my hair. What was I ever gonna do? All these words and sentences kept racing through my mind. I got up and paced the floor and tried to write things down but when I read them back out loud they all sounded like that word salad talk I heard back at Greil: *HOUSING LOW INCOME TRIANGULAR NOODLE AMBER ROD HAPPY TO BE HERE OH BROTHER.*

About 3 A.M. the wastebasket overflowed with crumpled-up notes so I turned my attention to painting the barn. Laying out one outfit after another, I thought I almost had one that looked halfway okay, but then my skirt didn't match my blouse and I really needed a different shade of lipstick and my shoes were way off and it was all wrong. A nervous fog descended on me and I could feel my blood pressure rising and I worried that with all the fuss I was making I might just lose my head completely and just walk out my door stark naked for all Washington, D.C., to gawk at and laugh.

I don't think sleep ever came.

Turns out the Senate building is everything you've seen it to be on TV. Inside that building they took me down front and had me sit at this long table. Everybody famous and powerful was already behind me seated up in chairs in row upon row of half circles. I recognized Senator Ted Kennedy's broad smile as I glanced around. A row of stern-looking men in dark suits sat before me, their water glasses sweating. In front of my face was a microphone I was supposed to speak into. I had never spoken into a microphone before. Someone got up and told everybody about the conference over at Howard University and what we were aiming to do to help improve the low-income-housing situation across the country. Then they introduced the representative from the conference, Martha Hawkins, from Montgomery, Alabama.

Whoa, that was me.

"Hello-o-ow, I'm so h-h-happy . . ." I began. My voice foghorned and made everybody jump. I was too close to the microphone. I stopped and backed away. Could I really do this? Seconds ticked as I tried to gather my reserve. Swallowing, I began to pray, God, really? Do you really want me here? Is this really part of your plan? All eyes in the Senate were locked on me now. The tension felt as thick as a cold bowl of gravy. Then came a voice. I was wondering if it was gonna show up. The words came in a flash and I recognized its strength immediately.

"Martha?" Suddenly we were away from it all, sitting in my kitchen, just the voice of love and me. We were breaking bread together, with lots of butter on it, and drinking tall glasses of sweet tea. I was about to help myself to another slice when the voice spoke again: "Martha, you have been anointed to preach good tidings to the meek. You have been sent to bind up the brokenhearted. Your purpose is to proclaim liberty to the captives and open the prisons of those that are bound." The words from Isaiah 61 came all in a burst.

"Why don't you have some more tea?" I said to the voice, and poured from the pitcher. "I could listen to you talk all day."

"Do you know why it's fitting that you are sitting in this Senate room with all these national dignitaries?" the voice asked. "It's the answer to that question I asked you months ago. This is your true identity Martha. You are a daughter of the King. I never want you to forget that. From lowly places I have raised you up. And now here you are on your Father's behalf. You are a daughter of the King—so speak now—and I will help you speak the words you need to say."

The kitchen vision disappeared in a flash and I was back in the Senate. It felt like no time had passed. "Hello, I'm so happy to be with you here today," I said into the microphone, and smiled. You could feel the whole room relax. "Thank you for giving us this opportunity to address you on the subject of low-income housing."

I don't remember exactly what I said after that, but my voice had an undeniable new clarity to it. I never looked at my notes once. They didn't make much sense anyway. My mouth simply opened and the words that needed to be said came forth. I spoke about what it was like to be in low-income housing, how it wasn't where I wanted to be, but it was a situation I got caught in and I was trying to make the best of it. I spoke of how other people can sometimes have a tendency to look down on you when you're in low-income housing and might not value you as a person or what you have to offer a community. But that's not a fair assessment of who you are. Your situation may simply be the hand you were dealt and might not reflect anything to do with your real self. I outlined some specifics of what might be done to help the situation, about how God's external opportunities extend to any willing heart, about how the same folks around this room who were charged with shaping the future were invited anew to step forward and lead boldly, to never lump people together by lack of wealth or color or faction or birth, and to continue caring for people anywhere who needed care. Those were the themes of what I said.

There was lots of applause afterward.

Later we went over to the cafeteria in the Capitol, the members of our group just happy and talking. They all said, you did good, girl, so good. Then we went back to our rooms over at Howard. It was quite a day.

About a month later the office of the president mailed me a big thick book. Mr. Reagan was leading the country then and his signature was in the book. Inside its pages were lists of groups and individuals all over the United States who were doing good work, a type of Who's Who of community volunteering. My name was listed in that book: Martha Hawkins. Martha Hawkins, daughter of the King. I said it out loud so I would never forget again.

14

The People
You'll Meet

WELL, THAT WAS SPEAKING AT the United States Senate.

Then real life came back to me. Back to the projects. Back to dreaming. Back to being broke. I was always broke. Broke. Broke. Broke. I started taking cakes around to different businesses and selling them. Pound cakes, mostly, those were the best sellers, and sometimes German chocolate cakes, those sold well too. Folks always like cake. Red velvet, coconut, chocolate fudge, pineapple upside down—I made them all. The pound cakes were crafted with black walnut flavoring and whipped cream; they came out of the oven golden yellow, fat and fluffy, and you could smell the country butter clear up to Chattanooga. Growed men in button-down suits tasted those cakes and smiled toothy grins like they was young boys again and said things like, "Oh, that's just melt-in-your-mouth good."

One of these button-down men I met was a Montgomery attorney named Calvin Pryor. He was an older black man nearing sixty with wiry hair, a salt-and-pepper mustache, and a wise squared-jaw face. He practiced law for the U.S. Department of Justice and soon became a dear friend. Mister Pryor believed we was living in good times. Things was changing for the better, and folks were seeing this good change come at a rapid pace. When Mister Pryor had started college in the late 1940s, there was only one black lawyer in the entire state of Alabama. By the time he finished law school in the early 1950s, there was ten. Now, mid- to late stride in his career in the late 1980s, he couldn't come close to counting them all. Shoot, he said, at the rate we were going you never knew what was possible—we might even see a black president someday.

Well, this next bit of information wasn't much his fault because the good attorney sat behind a desk all day, but as such he had an extra pound or two on him like many of us do. On the side I was selling a weight-loss formula. With all the cooking and eating I had done over the years I had fluffed out a bit as well and had used the product to drop a few pounds myself so I knowed it would work. Mister Pryor started buying weight-loss formula from me. Then as soon as he found out I sold pound cakes he appeared much more interested in that direction.

"This is a shame, Martha, a mighty shame." He scowled as I dropped off a double supply of weight-loss products and pound cake in his office. He eyed the cake more closely and grinned. "Whatcha trying to do to me anyway, Martha? With cakes like these, this business of selling weight-loss products doesn't seem to suit you much." He unwrapped the pound cake and sliced himself off a big piece.

"Well, it's not what I'm really doing for all times. It's just what I'm doing for now."

"Do tell," he said while getting busy with his teeth.

"I hope to own my own restaurant one day. All I need is a place I can afford."

"Starting up a restaurant isn't cheap. But I don't doubt that you'll get your place one day. Hard work, faith, and determination can accomplish most anything, and you seem to have all three in good amounts."

I smiled. "I'm not really looking at commercial sites, nothing like in a mall or corner pad or nothing. I want to get an old house and put my restaurant in that. My dream is to own a place where folks can come and feel like they're eating right in my home." He had told me before that he dabbled in real estate so I figured he might have some leads around the city.

Mister Pryor's eyes brightened at that last statement. "You know, Martha, I might just have the ideal place for you. There's a house I own downtown that's zoned commercially. It's a bit worn down but it would be perfect for what you're describing. Only problem is there's somebody else renting it right now, a day care center. They're good clients and appear to be long term, but if the place ever comes available I'll let you know."

Mister Pryor finished his slice and placed an order for another cake next week. Right after the talk I drove over to the address he had given me to take a look at the place. The house was run-down like he said, although it was colorful with kids' paintings in the windows and a friendly sign out front. The more closely I looked at the house's front it seemed to straighten itself up for inspection, as old as it was, like there was a moving of courage in the very rafters of that place. It was October 1986 and the leaves were still on the trees, not yet ready to fall, and they danced with possibility in the warm autumn air, golden red, golden orange, golden brown.

"Voice of love," I prayed, from behind the wheel of the Pinto. "I'm listening to you and I believe that's my house. I ain't aiming to put no day care center out on the street or nothing, so I pray they would find another spot that's gonna be more suitable for their needs. But that's my house—if that's truly what you're saying to me right now, I just know it in prayer. Someday that's gonna be my house."

The Red Sea didn't part. Time passed and when the house didn't open up after a couple of months I concluded that the voice of love was continuing with his humoring ways. My mind drifted to the hope of catering. When I took stock of my experience, it wasn't on the list yet. I had cooked for the SWEC conference and done my cakes and pies on the side, and done the all-you-can eat buffet at my house for folks to stop by and eat up, and taken lunches around to businesses, but I had never done any actual catering. I knew that a small restaurant would need to do both someday in order to survive—be a place for folks to come eat during the days, then be ready to take the food and the love out to larger groups on weekends. But I didn't know how to get started in catering or even what I needed, so I started asking the voice of love about it. For the time being, he was again staying silent.

Here's how this one worked out: while selling the pound cakes I met a man who owned a funeral home. Talking with him led to working part-time there for a spell, sitting at the front desk answering phones. Soon the funeral home man heard that a movie was coming to town. He knew some folks who knew some folks, and pretty soon I was talking with the people who were running the movie. They wanted real authentic soul food for all the cast and crew members while in Montgomery and they asked if I wanted the job. Yes I said yes I said yes I said yes.

So that was my first catering job, working for 20th Century Fox movie studies. Not a bad way to start out, I thought. True, I didn't have no business license or nothing and I didn't know nothing about actual catering; I just went over and cooked. The movie was called *Sister, Sister* and was written by Maya Angelou. It was about a reverend's family in the South who undergoes a heap of stress from their two daughters, Carolyne and Sissy Lovejoy. Staring in the movie was Diahann Caroll, Rosalind Cash, Irene Cara, and Paul Winfield. I

needed to be there every day to set the food out, so I ended up getting to know most of them folks.

My cooking for the movie served two purposes: to feed everybody, and to provide food for any eating scenes they needed.
One scene involved a church bazaar where they were selling food
and eating stuff. That day I fixed up two long tables, the first with
barbecued ribs, potato salad, candied yams, chitlins, fried chicken,
and collards, and the second with yellow cake, pink cake, green
cake, and mincemeat pies. I guess sometimes the food that's used for
shooting sits a long time and gets cold or sometimes it ain't even real
food, but as they were shooting this scene someone musta caught a
whiff of the ribs because he hollered out. "Hey, that's real food!" and
right away someone else hollered "Well glory be! Cut!" and for some
time after that it was all gobbling and munching at the tables while
I was running to and fro to replace whatever I could so the scene
could still be shot.

Come another afternoon I was restocking the cast and crew
table when a remarkable-looking woman with a dash of silver in her
hair walked over. I hadn't seen her on the set before, though she
looked a mite familiar. She wore big hoop earrings that sparkled and
a long brown-and-gold dress that reached to her feet.

"Hey, girl, good job with the cooking," the woman said. "I just
tried some of your fried chicken and it was delicious. I came back
looking for what you had in the way of dessert."

"Thank you, ma'am. Everybody seems to like the pound cake
real fine."

The woman picked up a piece and inhaled. "Mmmmmm, I can
just smell the butter. That's so-o-o-o good. You been working in
catering long?"

"No. Not long. Not long at all. But I've always loved to cook."

"Well, you're real smart at it. When you love to do something, it
becomes part of your life, doesn't it? Me, I make writing as much a
part of my life as I do eating or listening to music."

I looked at her more closely. She kept eating her cake.

"My name's Maya," she said, and gave me a little hug. "Thanks for what you're doing here."

"I'm Martha," I said. And the meeting was over. She evaporated into the crowd real sudden and I didn't see her no more on the set after that.

That lady was real gracious. She ate my cake and made me feel hopeful about the direction I was heading. One of the producers told me later who she was. I had savored her poems in the past and I was familiar with *I Know Why the Caged Bird Sings*, but I had never seen a picture of what she looked like in real life. That woman had come from mighty humble roots herself. She and her brother were abandoned by their parents when they were little and had traveled through much of their growing-up years like suitcases being passed back and forth between relatives. Things got much worse for her before they got better. But she came out the other side strong and confident and was doing real well for herself now. Real well.

When the shooting was over there was more movie work if I wanted it, first in Tuscaloosa and then in California, but I turned the movie folks down. Those places were too far away for me. Nyrone was still at home and graduating in a year or so and I didn't want to uproot him. So after all that catering business for the movie company and meeting Maya Angelou and all I went back on welfare and kept selling cakes and herbal supplements on the side.

In my spare time I kept volunteering. I was also upping the amount of books I read. Biographies of strong, capable women inspired me the most. I read all about Georgia Gilmore, an everyday woman like me who was just struggling to raise her children, make a living, and support her community like we all were. She ended up cooking for the movement in the 1950s. I had never met her personally but you heard her name around Montgomery from time to time. Reading about her life kept stoking the fires of my own dream.

Let me just tell you about her a minute. It seems that Missus Gilmore started out cooking behind the counter at the National Lunch Company on Court Street downtown but got herself fired because her boss heard that she had gone to court to testify on Mister King's behalf during the bus boycott. So that's when her cooking went underground. She gathered together a group of women unto her and they called themselves the Club from Nowhere. Their sole aim was to cook pies and cakes and sell them to raise money for the movement. She also cooked and brought huge tubs of food to the mass meetings. Maybe the strongest thing she's remembered for is opening her home to anybody in the movement who needed a safe place to eat. Her home wasn't advertised as a real restaurant—Missus Gilmore never called it one—everybody just said they was going down by Georgia's to eat. Reverend King was there often. He needed a place where he could trust the food, and Missus Gilmore supplied. She was known for plating him up with pork chops and stuffed bell peppers, it was said, and the reverend always asked for a second glass of her famed iced tea.

That flavor of what happened inside her walls was what inspired me most. 'Twas something special happening there. The folks writing about Missus Gilmore described meals around her table as more like being at a rally than a restaurant. The feeling in her home became downright sacramental, a camp meeting of sorts with a continual loud and loving conversation about the things that mattered. Folks would feel free to stand or sit or walk about from room to room with plates of food in their hands. It was the fact that a person's cooking could become so much more than just cooking—that's what I was aiming to do someday. By the time I read about her, Missus Gilmore was alive but she was getting on in years. She was rumored to still be around town. Her son, Mark Gilmore, was a city councilman. I didn't know how I could ever meet Missus Gilmore but I hoped I would one day.

"I remember the boycott really well," Calvin Pryor said to me one day. We was sitting in his law office and he was spooning up big pieces of the pound cake I had just brought him. "You know, I'm good friends with Fred Gray, the attorney who worked with Rosa and Martin. We all knew Georgia Gilmore and what she was doing in her home for the movement." Mister Pryor was eating slower than usual, savoring up each spoonful.

"Any word on the house opening up?" I asked.

"Day care center's still in it. They good renters. I don't think they'll be leaving anytime soon."

"I been thinking about it a lot, you know." I started gathering my things to leave.

Mister Pryor set down his plate and got a preaching look on his face. "Martha, you don't let go of your dream easily—I see that about you. More people need what's driving you. When folks face hardships they need to know that those things are sometimes not a curse but a blessing. They can make you stronger. Like I said, if ever that house becomes available, you'll be the first to know."

Now, Calvin Pryor was a good man. He talked sense and he liked my cakes just fine. But there were a few things that Calvin Pryor didn't know about me. Mainly, that I didn't have no money. And when I say no money, I'm talking *none*. But that wasn't stopping the Spirit of courage from stirring the waters because about a week later Mister Pryor phoned me up. "Martha? You still interested in that house?"

"You know I am."

"I never thought this would happen, but the day care center's leaving. . . ."

"Do tell."

"I'll be honest here, Martha. I can't put any money into the house right now and I'm renting it as is. If you want it you'll need to fix it up some. But if you do that you can have the first three months rent free. How's that sound to you?"

I took a deep breath, trying hard not to scream for happiness. It was October 1987, exactly one year after Mister Pryor first told me about the house. I chose my words carefully, trying to sound all businesslike. "Well, yes, I believe I can enter into that agreement." The next day I went down to the law office and signed the rental agreement: *Martha Hawkins*. The house was mine—for at least three months, anyway. That was all I needed to make things come about. My restaurant was finally going to happen!

After signing the papers I sped over there by myself to check out the house. Do you know that feeling when you stick a big wedge of baker's chocolate in a pot to melt? It sort of slides down all distasteful and sits there with a plop yearning for something to come make it sweet. That's how I felt as I surveyed the joint with a closer eye to what needed to be done. Everywhere outside needed painting. Boards and shutters hung loose. Grass and shrubs were overgrowed. Inside was a mess. Kids' wallpaper was stuck to every room. All interior walls needed new paint. Mounds of tape were stuck fast to windows and floors. The plumbing leaked, and I had heard somewhere that you need two bathrooms to open a restaurant—there was only one. The kitchen area was far too small to be used commercially. There was one apartment-sized oven and a tiny old fridge that looked like it should be thrown out. No Holy Spirit was sparkling in the floorboards today, that was for sure. What had I gotten myself into? Gathering a scrap of paper and a pencil I started scribbling, adding up what I'd need to open. The dollar signs flashed hard in my head. I'd need money for:

> permits and licenses
> insurance
> business and occupation taxes
> monthly rent once the three free months was up
> a heap of cleaning supplies to scour the joint
> commercial-grade pots and pans
> industrial-grade kitchen appliances
> a three-compartment sink
> a deep fryer and ice machine
> a hood and ventilation system for the kitchen
> a complete new bathroom
> an upgrade of the old one
> new paint inside and out

various structural repairs throughout to get things
up to code
a new sign out front
new lighting
supper tables and chairs
cups, saucers, silverware
aprons, tablecloths, napkins, curtains, and service
cloths
printed menus
advertising costs to get word out before opening
a cash register

The bottom line flared up like a grease fire with no salt on hand to put it out.

Fifty thousand dollars.

That's what it was going to take to open my restaurant. It might have well have been fifty million. Hoo boy. That baker's chocolate needed a heap of sugar to make it sweet. What, oh what had I gotten myself into? I called my sister Rosa and asked her to come by and take a look at things. She was always real good about assessing a situation. Rosa rolled on over and rolled on by. From her house she called me back. "Yep, that's one big old raggly building you got there," she said.

That was it.

My crying and moaning lasted a total of five minutes. Or ten. Okay, maybe twenty. But then I dried my tears and decided to push forward with everything I had. I knew a thing or two about falling back on sheer determination and if that's what it would take, that's what I'd do. I called everyone I knew and invited them to a fixing-up party. I'd supply the paint and a big meal if they supplied elbow grease. In the days to come I cooked up some cakes and pies, sold them, and bought paint and brushes. I asked everybody I knew to bring to the party the hammers and saws they already owned.

The day of the party came. The hour came when everybody was supposed to show. Nobody came. That hour ticked by. Then another. Then one person showed up. He came through the front door, walked around while looking at the walls and ceilings, then stood in the front room, silent. "It don't look like nobody's coming," he said. "I'll come back tomorrow." He walked out. Guess his tomorrow never came cause he never came back.

The evening after the painting party that never was, I went home crushed. Lying down on my bed, I began to think. I knew plenty of folks loved me, I didn't doubt that. Folks get busy and have jobs during the day and there's always a heap of other things to do, so I didn't blame them. In fact, it made sense for them not to put much stock in this—on paper my restaurant did look like a crazy idea. I had a history with craziness, too—it would have made sense for people to think I was falling off the deep end again. Who was I fooling? I didn't have no money. I didn't have no business smarts. I didn't have nothing. If just one person would show up and stay to help, even for a day, maybe that's all it would take to get the ball rolling. That's all the sign I would need that this thing would succeed. I prayed all that night. That's all I did was pray.

Toward morning clarity came and I realized what was missing. "Voice of love," I prayed. "I forgot that this restaurant ain't gonna be all about me. I've got my determination and I'm willing to work hard. But it ain't gonna be sheer determination that opens this thing up. There's no way this thing can open unless you show up and help."

Later that morning I was back in the old house wondering what to do when one of my son's friends knocked on the door. He had his hands in his pockets and when he came inside he sort of shrugged and grinned. "Hey, I'll help," he said.

We got to work.

He didn't stay long but he didn't need to. God hadn't left me alone, I knew that now, so I kept baking cakes and pies, buying one bucket of paint at a time, just figuring things out as I went along.

The painting went pretty easy. Scraping all that old wallpaper off proved another matter. Scraping off old wallpaper turns saints into sinners. Every weekend I scrounged around at garage sales and bought old pots and pans, silverware, tables, mixed-matched sets of dishes—anything I could find that would prove useful. Then, it was a grand day when I had finally saved up enough to get my sign out front: MARTHA'S PLACE CATERING AND RESTAURANT. From that day on I looked at it every day to remind me afresh of what I was doing. It was the sign of the dream that was keeping me going. It would have been easy to stop again and say I couldn't do this. But I kept in mind how things could be, not how it was. That thought kept me going.

The three months of free rent was long since up but I was far from opening my doors. I have no money other than my welfare check, so I moved out of Cedar Park and into the upstairs of the old house. Nyrone, my youngest, had left for college that September so it was just me at home now. If the restaurant failed completely I could always fall back and get a full-time job somewhere, but I didn't know where. Maybe back at the glass factory, but I sure didn't want to go back there again. I was so close to my dream. So close. Every dime I had went into opening that restaurant.

Well, the winter winds starting blowing in and around that old house, and the heat wasn't turned on yet, so I moved my bedroll downstairs at night so I could sleep. Opening the door to that old stove, I turned the gas up and lay in the glow of that oven. My backside warmed up but then my front froze. So I turned over and it was the reverse. I kept rolling all night like a chicken on a spit. Never did sleep much.

One day in early spring I heard a knock on the door. It was a man named Craig Conwell, a businessman from across the street. We had said hello to each other a couple of times. He had seen my sign out front and knew a restaurant was coming soon. "Hey," Craig said. "we want to know if we can come eat. Can we make a reservation?"

I had paint in my hair and was moving a box of silverware I had just picked up. I must not have been thinking straight. "Sure," I said. "Uh . . . when do you want to come?"

"Tomorrow."

"Tomorrow? Oh, okay. How many?

"Reservation for twenty. About eleven thirty. We're right across the street. That work for you?"

"Um . . . I can do that."

So just like that I was open for business. But not really. Not officially. Not legally. I figured this thing for Craig would be a onetime event. Sort of a catering thing in an old abandoned house. Yeah. That was it. They'd eat and I'd make some more money for more paint. Then I could keep going on the original schedule.

My niece came over the next day and helped out. We cooked all morning and set out a big buffet for the party. We had gotten the front room scrubbed up at least and shined the floor. (There were three main eating areas on the ground floor—a front room and two side rooms.) My niece sewed up some curtains. I set up five old tables I had scrounged and chairs, and put some fresh flowers on each table. Nothing else. Just before they came, my niece and I held hands and prayed. "Lord Jesus, I don't know if this is entirely right what I'm doing here, following the spirit of the law and not the letter, but I ask that you would see though our shortcomings and bless this day. Please bless the food we're about to serve and all the folks who come and partake of it. Amen."

Well, Craig and his party came and they seemed to enjoy things just fine. We breathed a sigh of relief. Mostly relief, anyway. I still worried I would be going to jail. The morning after the party we got another phone call. It was a coworker from Craig's office. "Yeah, hey," he said. "Craig put a sign up on the bulletin board here in the office that says your restaurant is serving up great food. Can we make a reservation for lunch today? Party of four."

"Yes," I said, and gulped. There was that one little word again that sets everything in motion. Word was out now, but I didn't know if I wanted it to be out. Craig just thought he was helping out my business. He didn't know we weren't officially open yet. The party of four came by that day and we served them. The next day three fellas came in and wanted lunches to go. I fixed them up some chicken and corn bread I had back in the fridge. They seemed to like that fine because the phone rang the day after that, and the day after that, but by then my conscience was kicking up a storm so I stopped answering the phone. "Lord Jesus," I prayed. "I'm crying out to you, Lord. We got a dream going here. But I can't do anything about it. Can you please just open the doors and make a way to open the restaurant and make it legal?"

Sophia Bracy Harris stopped by one afternoon to see what I was up to. She came through the front door and let out a low whistle. "Well, I heard it was happening but I had to see it with my own eyes. This is really starting to take shape."

"Sophia, I still got a long, long ways to go. You know anywhere I can get about fifty thousand dollars?" I got down to business right away.

She smiled and shook her head. "Not that much, no. What did they say at the bank when you went in?"

"The bank?" (You have to realize I was *that* clueless.)

Sophia looked at me more closely. "You know, for a business loan. You draw up a plan that shows what you're going to do and how you're going to make money. If they think it's a sound business plan, they loan you the money."

"Will that work?"

Sophia thought for a moment. "You know, we've been thinking lately that FOCAL is not only interested in child care but in helping women succeed as well. We haven't actually helped any women yet with the program, but you could be our first. Let me put you in contact with my assistant. She'll help you draw up a business plan."

I shrugged. "I'm sure game if you're game."

"You're going to open this restaurant soon." Sophia gave me a hug and handed me the number for her assistant. "I know you can do it. Let me know how it goes with the bank."

So just like that, with Sophia Harris's assistant's carefully drawn up business plan in hand, I headed over to the bank. I had been fixing up the old house for about ten months by now.

Two middle-aged men looked over my plan. They both wore dark suits and had half-glasses sitting far down their noses. Their faces looked stern.

"Business loan, hmmm?" said the first. "It says on your application that you're on welfare. We're wondering what sort of collateral you might have?"

"Co-co-collaturalls?" I said. "What's that?"

The man to my right looked over his glasses at me for a few moments without saying anything. "Ma'am, you need to own something before our bank will lend you money. If you default on your loan, the bank keeps your collateral."

I nodded like I knew.

"So, the collateral?"

I shook my head. I didn't have nothing.

The bankers glanced at each other. The first rummaged through some papers on his desk and cleared his throat. The second closed my file and handed it back to me. "I'm sorry, Missus Hawkins, but restaurants are considered very high-risk businesses. Ninety percent fail within their first year. The bank would be afraid that you would have difficulties paying us back."

They were nice fellas doing their jobs. I shook hands and left, figuring that would be the end of things. But that evening one of the bankers called me back with excitement in his voice. "Missus Hawkins, I talked to my boss over at the main branch. Your application was really unique, we don't see many like that around here, and our boss was quite intrigued by your story. Would you be able to meet us all down at the downtown branch tomorrow at nine A.M.?"

"Sure. What about?"

"Well, we'd rather explain it to you tomorrow."

Next morning the three men sat in front of me behind the same desk. They were all grins. The two younger fellas sat on either side. The boss sat in the middle. He was older and looked like he was all business. The boss spoke first. "Missus Hawkins, we went through your application again and were quite impressed with your drive and determination. We've talked it through and have a proposition for you."

I nodded.

"As a bank, we're unable to loan you money because you simply don't meet our criteria. Rules are rules and in this case we can't bend them. But what we can do is invest in your business personally. We are interested in seeing the city succeed and so we'd like to offer you a sixty-forty partnership. We're prepared to invest the money up front to ensure your restaurant gets off on sound footing."

I leaned forward, all ears. "Sixty-forty partnership? Can you explain that more?"

"It means that we will own the majority interest in your restaurant. It's a sound business decision, and arrangements like this are established all the time. We'll help you get up and running, and when profits begin to roll in—and we expect they will—you'll pass along to us our portion of the proceeds."

My head spun at the possibility. "Out of curiosity," I said, "how much money were you thinking of investing in my restaurant?"

"Well"—here one of the younger bankers spoke. "Just so you know, technically it would be *our* restaurant. And we want to see our investment succeed, Missus Hawkins, so we're prepared to offer you"—he glanced from left to right then back at me and whispered the next words—"fifty thousand dollars."

I hoped they didn't hear me gasp. I could be officially open in two weeks! Maybe quicker. I could buy all my commercial appliances. I could put in that new bathroom. I could even hire help! The men sat before me. They were all smiles. One of the young bankers opened a file. "We have the paperwork all drawn up for

you, Missus Hawkins. You just need to sign here, here, and here."
He pointed.

I didn't hesitate with my decision. I looked at the men as grate-fully and sincerely as I could. "Thanks so much for this offer," I said.
"But my answer is no."

15

My Crazy Dream

"WHY?" ROSA SAID. MY SISTER was helping me pull weeds in the front yard of the old house. It was late September 1988, not long after the meeting at the bank, and the Alabama sun was still thinking it was summer although it wasn't yet noon. "Martha, you turned down a heap of money. It would have solved all your problems, girl."

I wiped my brow. "I got my reasons."

Rosa shook her head and kept pulling. "You gonna let anybody else in on those reasons? Everybody thinks you've gone plumb crazy again to turn down big cash money like that."

"Well, it's because it wouldn't have been mine. Those other fellas would've owned it."

"Yours? Why does that matter?"

I sighed and wiped the dirt off my hands. "That's always been the shape of the dream. To own and run the restaurant myself. It was gonna be *Martha's Place*, and that sign out front was gonna mean something in how things was gonna flow. To get my restaurant up and running it had to be God making it happen, and it had to be me not being desperate. That was the way it had to be."

"Well, the way you're talking now sounds like that big old dream of yours might be all behind you, Martha."

I went back to pulling. "It might just be, Rosa. It might just be."

For some time there was only the sound of rearranging dirt, of clods getting shaken from roots, of roots getting tossed in an old tin bucket. Rosa must have been figuring through things in her head because after some time she sat up from where she had crouched by the shrub bed and asked, "So if things might be all behind you, how come you're still pulling weeds?"

I needed to think about that one for a while too. If I had been fool enough to turn down an offer as good as that I might as well just pack up and go home. I patted the dirt, ready for some flowers we was gonna plant as soon as I got some more money. At last I said, "I guess I'm still pulling weeds because I still got a little faith."

A phone started ringing from somewhere inside the old house. I dusted myself off and went inside to answer it. Sophia Bracy Harris was on the line. "Martha, can you meet today for lunch?" she said. "There's something I need to talk to you about. How about Cracker Barrel, around twelve thirty?"

"Sounds good," I said. "See you then."

Sophia was already browsing in the country store section of Cracker Barrel when I arrived. She was standing next to a display of vintage cans and food packages. "Look at this antique container," she said and pointed to a yellow-and-red tin pail about the size of two ice cream buckets placed on top of each other. "Partridge brand pure lard. They don't make great old tins like this anymore, do they?"

I laughed and shook my head. "You think we're getting too old for today's world? All my boys are out of the house now, you know. I'm an empty nester, whatever that's supposed to mean."

"Girl, you're only forty-one," Sophia said. "And I'm not much off that. We've got lots of time left to do great things with our lives."

I gave her a little hug. "You're already doing them, Sophia. Hey, let's go get something to eat."

Sophia hugged me back and we got in line to be seated. Background restaurant noise swirled around us while we settled into our booth and started looking over the menu. Sophia nodded at her selection choice, then set hers down. I could tell she had something deep she wanted to ponder with me. "Martha, this is what I want to know about your decision," she said, and looked around at the packed restaurant. "Cracker Barrel did it all right. They saw mealtimes as more than just eating, maybe a chance to catch up with family and friends or your thoughts—and what they created is working for them. Just look at the crowd. They're like this every day."

"I know. I love this place," I said to Sophia, and then, "Farm-raised catfish, please, with a large iced tea," to the waitress, who had come to take our order.

"Chicken and dumplings, "Sophia said, "with a side of greens and a side of pintos." She smiled pleasantly and the waitress left to put in our order. Sophia breathed in like she had another mouthful to say. "They've got investors here, Martha. And they know that meals weren't meant to be swallowed down in three bites with a squirt of ketchup. So if they're making it happen here, why'd you turn down those big-money investors for your place?"

I sighed and looked out the window, thinking of how to explain my reasoning. "It was gonna be a different bottom line with those fellas from the bank, Sophia. I could just feel it. That's why. I ain't in this to make money, not big money, anyway. It would be nice if it came along once in a while, but that's not what I'm all about, that's not my bottom line. Some folks can make that work for them, and I'm happy for them, but that ain't me. I just want to run my business on my terms."

"What might those terms be, Martha?"

"Well, giving people second chances, I guess. Like I had given to me. Those terms can't be pushed by dollars." The ideas took solid shapes in my mind as I spread words over them. "The folks who work for me, the folks who come in to eat—if they've been out getting lost then they're invited to come to my restaurant and feel like they're home again. I don't rightly know how to explain it better than that."

"Those can be tall orders, Martha. And when you lay your foundations on those terms, you've got to abide by them later on, you know."

I nodded. "I know."

Sophia smiled. "That's what I like about you, Martha. Because I know you're going to run your restaurant your way when it opens." She slid a manila envelope across the table to me.

"What's up with this?" I asked.

"Well, it's not fifty thousand dollars. It's five. Do you think you could get your restaurant up and running with five thousand dollars?"

My mouth flew open. "What you talking about, girl? This isn't your money, is it?"

"No. And it's not a handout either. Half of it is a grant from FOCAL that's yours to keep. The other half is a loan that you'll repay one day. No hurry, either. This money is from people who believe in you, Martha. We want you to succeed and we believe you can—on your terms. We want you to make this restaurant come alive the way you've always envisioned it would." She smiled, her eyes sparkling.

I closed my mouth. The envelope felt heavy in my hands. Not a bad heavy. More a rich heavy. It felt like the weight of a dream was being lifted off my shoulders and being carried by more than one person now. For about two minutes I just sat and looked at that envelope, shaking my head in disbelief.

"How do I ever repay you for this kindness?" I asked finally.

"Someday you tell your story, Martha," Sophia said. "Tell people what it's been like for you so that others will recognize they can have dreams and begin to follow those dreams no matter what they've been through."

There was more talk after that, more smiling and laughing, more joy when the food arrived shortly after. Then a few days later some of the women from FOCAL got their husbands to come by the old house and install a second bathroom. They hammered and sawed and stuck up sheetrock and light fixtures. Women from the community who I didn't even know came and brought serving trays and shelves to put stuff on. A local doctor and his wife donated a whole bundle of fixings. A girl I knowed from school, Diane Hawkins, she had been just like a sister to me and had become Edward's wife, came by with an extra check for $2,000. A whole heap of folks came and went. All was a flurry of sweeping and polishing and mending and dreaming. Folks were digging in and helping out and I wasn't gonna let them down, no sir.

I went uptown to city hall to get my business license and sign the forms and take care of all the legal stuff. The good folks in city hall had seen my sign out front for months now and wondered when the doors were finally going to open, I guessed, because on the way in I could hear them whispering, Hey that's Martha, from Martha's Place—we've been wondering when she was ever gonna come in. I signed the papers and paid my fees and then—no joke—the people at city hall all started clapping. They stood up behind their desks and smiled and waved and cheered like I had been hired as head chef of the Bellagio Hotel.

Walking out of city hall, I grinned ear to ear, each step feeling a mile off the ground. My restaurant was official. My lifelong dream. Martha Hawkins, high school dropout, welfare mama, mental hospital patient—that young girl who had made so many mistakes had come a long, long way. Now it was Martha Hawkins, business owner, restaurateur, Senate speaker, daughter of the King. All odds had once been stacked against my success, but the voice of love had lifted me up from lowly places, and Martha's Place Restaurant & Catering had officially come to be.

We opened the front doors to my restaurant on October 17, 1988, a full two years after Calvin Pryor first told me about the old house, a full twelve months after I took the lease and started working on the house to fix it up. It was Nyrone's nineteenth birthday, too, a very good day. As a first order of business, the coach from Memphis came down and right there in the restaurant he signed up Nyrone to play football. Other folks filed in and ate. One man had kept my card for more than a year, just waiting for me to open. Another man ate, ordered seconds, wiped his mouth, then asked if he could bring his wife on down to take cooking lessons from me. I laughed and said sure. On the menu that day was steak and gravy, fried chicken, pork chop casserole, chicken and dumplings, baked ham, collards, chitlins, black-eyed peas, fried green tomatoes, sweet potato pie, peach cobbler, strawberry pie and, yes, pound cake—all the comfort foods that people love—*soul food* cuisine, as it's knowed around here. I just called it good things to eat.

In the weeks to follow, one of my first customers was a stooped woman with large dark-rimmed glasses and a red scarf tied around her neck. She was carrying a book about Nelson Mandela, and when she sat at a table and ordered fried chicken with chitlins I had to hold myself back from hugging her outright.

"This is mighty good food," she said after she had eaten, and then motioned me closer so she could speak into my ear. "This is the food that will sustain you," she said and gave my hand a little squeeze. Her voice flowed like the sound of rushing waters, a mighty river that rolled down and burbled on and on. She promised she'd be back soon, and promised she'd be bringing her friends next time. Then she took corn bread muffins to go, she did. From that day forward, anytime she came to my restaurant, Rosa Parks always took corn bread muffins to go.

Another man happened by soon and I recognized him as well.

It was Mark Gilmore, Montgomery city councilman. He ordered pork chop casserole with greens, lima beans, and sweet tea to drink.

"Your mama has been a real inspiration to me," I said to Mister Gilmore. "How's she doing, anyway?" I hoped I wasn't being presumptuous, asking about a legend like her in that way.

"Well, she's been getting on in years," he said, "but she's strong. Real strong. She's stopped cooking, you know—that's why I'm here today. This is some fine food you've got going here." He chewed for a while, thinking. "Hey, how'd you like to give my mama a call sometime? I think she'd enjoy hearing about what you've got going down here."

So, with much thanks to her son, I phoned up Missus Georgia Gilmore. I told her how much I admired her and what she had done for the movement, and about how she had provided a good deal of my inspiration for running an old restaurant, especially in a house. We talked for some time about this and that. Then she told me how to make her famous ice tea, the kind that Martin Luther King used to ask for seconds on. The secret's all in the boiling, Missus Gilmore said. You boil sugar and water together first, the day before you want to serve it, then you put the tea bags in a pitcher with aluminum foil on top. The next day you take the tea bags out, add water, and "just drink 'til you're tired. You can't have just one glass, you know, Martha. You will never want to stop drinking tea." That's what she said to me, her voice all sassy and free.

Those first few months were mostly a blur. Folks filed in and out and I cooked and served and moved as if in a dream. It wasn't big crowds that came. Not at first, anyway. The Christmas season came and went and it was real good and I paid the rent okay. I catered and stayed up all night sometimes, cooking, washing dishes, cleaning things up, and then getting ready for the next day to come. January came and cold weather with it, and folks across the city all decided in a bunch to stay home where it was warm. February came and went too and the cash flow tightened up. Regulars were making this their home already, but there wasn't enough regulars yet to carry me through if the crowds stayed lean like this.

So I prayed.

I knew a guy at the radio. He liked the food just fine and told the newspaper about the restaurant, the *Montgomery Advertiser*—it was right around the corner from me. A real nice reporter phoned me up and asked if she could do my story. I wasn't aware of how those things worked so, like a novice, I said I'm too busy. It was true—I had cooking to do, I couldn't be talking to no reporter, and I didn't have no money for advertising, if that's what she was trying to sell me.

But this was a news feature story and it wasn't gonna cost me nothing. Just like the workings of grace, all I had to do was say yes and the blessing would come my way. The reporter offered to come anytime convenient for me. I said the only time was 6:30 A.M., thinking she'd not come and I could keep going with my shy ways. But she said yes and she came at that early hour. We talked, she wrote the story, and soon after that a big spread appeared in the newspaper about the little restaurant where dreams come true.

Funny what a little publicity can do. After the newspaper story came out we had folks coming to the restaurant from all over the state—Elmore County, Macon County, Chilton, and Shelby. A man and his wife came down from Jackson, which is clear on the Tennessee border. Another couple came from Chocktaw, which borders Mississippi. We started having whole busloads of folks stop by. Tours of the Deep South. Folks was lining up every lunchtime now. One day I counted a hundred hungry people waiting to get in. It was worth the wait, said the man at the end of the line after he had eaten. We fed them all that day and the next and the next and the next. Weeks went by and then months, and folks came and ate and left as happy as hay.

About then is when I started to realizing I had a real restaurant. With all those dishes clanging and folks eating and smiling, I knew my dream had become reality. This is what I had been waiting to do since I was a little girl. It was my destiny. And we were gonna make it. This restaurant was gonna succeed. I had paid back the loan from Sophia. I had stepped into God's promise for my life and come home at last. It was good. Real good. Yes sir, it was.

There's one more story I need to tell you, though. It's a funny thing when you make great boasts about the terms of your business. My restaurant became mine because I wanted to run it a certain way. That's what Sophia had pressed me on that day at Cracker Barrel. But other folks will press you much harder on what you hold important if you let them. Folks will look to hurt you even, and sometimes they'll hold your hand to a stove and let it burn. I'd meet one of those folks soon enough. He'd charm his way into my restaurant and push and push against my terms of operation. My question was if I was gonna fold on what mattered most.

16

The Terms of Grace

THE RESTAURANT HAD BEEN OPEN for three years and I had developed a habit of bringing home strays whenever I saw one fall from the nest. A number of women I had met from ministering down at the prison came to me on work-release programs. One of my nephews got caught up in drugs and went into rehab, then worked for me for some time until he was able to get back on his feet again. Welfare moms, folks struggling with addictions, folks down on their luck—when it came to family or making ends meet, it didn't matter to me where they had been or what had happened to them or what they had done. I hired most anybody who needed help. Some folks stayed a week. Others a month or two. Others took a while longer to get up and around again. I figured that folks feel better about themselves when they're doing something useful with their time, and in my book nothing feels better than serving in a restaurant.

One of those strays was Richard. He was a thickset boy in his early twenties, about the same age as my sons. He had been staying in a homeless shelter up the road for the past few months when the shelter director brought him down to my restaurant one afternoon and said, "Hey, Martha, I think we got a worker for you." I was cleaning pans in the kitchen and we had just finished serving up a lunch rush from a tour bus. "What do you think, Richard?" I asked. "You want to work here at Martha's Place?"

"I can do most anything when I put my mind to it," he said. He had a thick neck like he had been lugging around alfalfa bales, and he was almost bald on top, as young as he was. On his chin he wore a scrubby goatee and had big whiskey-colored eyes, so big they seemed awash in his head.

I told him how things flowed around here and then I hugged him aboard. He kind of winced when I did that, like he wasn't used to that sort of thing, but that's how I always greeted any new worker in my restaurant. There's always a heap of folks in this world who are running short on hugs and I had found that some startling results can yield forth from that one simple action.

Richard soon proved a good worker. He kept his hours and scrubbed the pots hard. Sometimes he sang to himself if he thought I wasn't listening, simple songs about this and that—*This little light of mine, I'm gonna let it shine*, songs he must have learned somewhere when he was a kid.

"What's your story, anyway?" I asked Richard late one afternoon as we was clearing up tables after a shift. I had a pretty good hunch what it was but I wanted to hear things direct from him. I had come to learn that telling your story can have a powerful way of releasing what holds you down.

"Drugs," he said. "I used to use every day. Crack, mostly."

"How'd you get by?"

He tried to smile but it came out scrawny. "Well, I worked at first. Labor jobs, digging ditches, framing houses, whatever the day held. But time went on and I started using more and I was supporting my own habit, so keeping steady employment was tough. I got to where I was selling the stuff, stealing things, whatever I could find to turn a buck. Shoot, if I saw a lawn mower in someone's yard I'd take it. Things got pretty bad at the end. Before I went to live in the homeless shelter I was staying in an abandoned house." He shivered and looked away.

It wasn't an unusual story. Whenever drugs are being devoured I heard folks say similar things. That image of him staying in an abandoned house made me think real quick. "Say, Richard, when was the last time you stayed over in a real house, anyway?"

"What do you mean, Miz Hawkins?"

"Well, my boys are all gonna be home this weekend. Why don't you come on over and stay with us for a while. We'd like it if you did that."

His eyes changed from wide to faraway and he nodded. "It's been a long time since I been in a real home."

So Richard came and stayed with us. My boys were in and out around then and they was plenty big enough if something came up, but I wasn't worried much. A relapse was a real possibility, but when a person's been sleeping in shelters for a time there's often a genuine meekness that comes over him. You're showing him a light at the end of his tunnel, a remembrance of the way things were once. Maybe even a hope of the way things could be again.

We held family Bible studies in the living room and Richard joined us, savoring up the Word of God. We had a guest room and Richard slept in there. I drove him in to work each morning and back home again each night. About two weeks into his stay I was doing laundry at home and noticed that his bed hadn't been slept in though he had been home every night in his room. I went out to the living room where he was reading his Bible. "Richard, you been sleeping standing straight up?" I asked.

"No ma'am."

"Then what gives with the clean sheets?"

"Well, uh . . ." He kind of looked away. "I been on the floor."

"How come, child? The Lord's given you a perfectly good bed to use. Why don't you get some good rest in it?"

He looked back, his jaw beginning to tremble. "Well, ma'am, it just didn't seem right."

"Speak to me, Richard. What's scaring you away?"

"Well, I guess I'm just not adjusted to all this love. That's why I've been sleeping on the floor. Is that all right with you if I keep doing that?"

I hugged the boy. Of course it was all right. Richard wasn't blindsiding me. He was walking straight and we both knew it. By then he had been sober for more than a year. Whatever made him most at ease was okay by me.

Richard stayed in the guest room for several months, all the while sleeping on the floor. I opened a second restaurant location around then in a Ramada Hotel near Hope Hull out by the airport. Richard worked both locations, washing dishes, cooking from my recipes, carrying the food out to the customers. Things started going better for him all around. He had been staying clean and saving his money, enough so that he was able to afford his own apartment. That was a good day for Richard, when he was finally able to stand on his own again. The apartment was gonna be a bit of a stretch for him, so he took on a second job running a filling station over yonder in town. He was keeping his hours at the restaurant and working hard, so I figured it must have been the right choice.

All was going well until one day Richard didn't show up for his shift. I phoned his apartment but there was no answer. I must admit I got to worrying overnight about that. "Where you been?" I asked the next morning when he showed up.

Richard lowered his face. "I stayed over at my girlfriend's, ma'am. I'm sorry, Miz Hawkins. We just lost track of time. I didn't want to come in late to work so I just stayed away. It won't happen again. Honest."

I looked at him real closely. As I was looking, as careful as I could, I sniffed. "You been drinking?" I asked. I wasn't asking to judge. I wanted to know what kind of situation I was dealing with.

"No, ma'am," he said. "My girlfriend had a glass of wine and some got spilled on my jacket. That's all."

I looked at him real close again. We looked at each other for a clear two minutes without saying anything. Finally I gave him a hug. "Well, you best get in the kitchen then. Dishes won't wash themselves."

Shortly after that he asked to borrow my car so he could go cash a check. I let him. The bank was just down the street but three hours later he was still gone. I closed the restaurant after the lunch rush cleared out and caught a ride home with Rosa. That night I wasn't sure what I should do. Should I phone the police, or should I just wait it out?

Richard came back to the restaurant early next morning. He needed to do some things with my car, he said, and he was mighty sorry. There was lots of talk and even some tears and all, but I was starting to have some grave doubts. That was Richard's second chance, and he had blown it, big time.

'Twas about a week later, March 1, 1993, to be exact, when I showed up for work at 4 A.M. as usual, and the front door to Martha's Place was jimmied wide open, swinging loose on its hinges. I hurried inside, took a sharp look around, and phoned the police. They came right away and asked questions about this and that. Three hundred dollars was missing from the cash register, though everything else looked in order. Come 8 A.M. Richard didn't show up for his shift. I knew the truth then.

About 2 P.M. the police phoned me. Richard was downtown in lockup, asking for me. Did I want to come talk? I said okay, but I was shorthanded thanks to Richard. I needed to finish cleaning up the tables and getting ready for the next day. About two hours later I went downtown.

County jail is everything they say it is. It's cement blocks and iron bars and cold floors and the place where only country songs get birthed. I'm thankful I ain't never been behind bars myself, but I know that cold feeling of not being free. A guard ushered me back to where Richard was lying on a bunk facedown. I paused in front of his bars for a moment, not knowing if he was passed out or sleeping.

"Get up, you skunk," the guard barked. "Scum like you'se gonna stand when folks wanna talk to you."

I laid my hand on the guard's arm. "Thank you, sir. Would I be able to talk to him alone for a spell?"

"Five minutes. I'll be behind the door if you need anything."

Richard was on his feet now. He stood about a yard back from the bars, hands in his pockets, looking at the floor. His clothes were torn and smudged with dirt stains. Dark circles lay heavy underneath his eyes.

"What's been going on?" I asked. I didn't quite know where to begin with him.

"It was me, you know," he said. "I robbed your restaurant."

"Yeah, I figured that much."

"I met some guys downtown last night. We were just drinking at first. Then they went out back of the bar and they said for me to come along. One of the fellas fired up a rod—you know, lit up a crack pipe—and when that scent hit my nose it was like all those days on the pipe came back in a flash. I wanted more drugs right away, so I went and bought eight balls for eighty bucks, about three grams. That was all the money I had on me, and I smoked it all right then and wanted more. I went back to the filling station where I work and took a hundred and fifty bucks from there and got some more crack. I smoked that. Then I went to another filling station, the one near Fairview, and I robbed that and bought more crack. But it still wasn't enough. I knew you kept some petty cash in the restaurant, so I broke in through the front door and took that." His

words were racing out all at once and he needed to take a breath to
continue.

"What you gonna do now?" I asked.

He kept his gaze low. "You know, Miz Hawkins, when I robbed
that last gas station I didn't have no gun on me or nothing. I just
walked in and said, 'Hand me the money.' There was a woman and
a man in there and they gave it over without saying a word. They
looked so scared, you know. But I wasn't gonna hurt them. Maybe I
was. I don't know. I was coming down then. Really starting to feel it.
I suppose I could've done anything."

"It still wasn't enough?"

"Well, it was four o'clock in the morning and I was crashing
hard. I didn't know where I could get any more drugs after that.
Here's the troubling thing, Miz Hawkins—strong as the urge still
was, my conscience was working real thick in me too. All I could
think about was that I had robbed Martha. You were the only one
who ever cared for me. You took me in. You showed me love and
treated me like a blood son. That was the shame I was feeling."

Our five minutes was up and the guard came back and said I
needed to leave. I didn't know what to say to Richard. Maybe I
wasn't supposed to say nothing. I think he had spoken his peace.

A couple of months later they took Richard before the judge.
Turned out that a woman was helping him when he had robbed the
last store and she was holding a gun in her purse. Richard didn't tell
me that. When they arrested Richard, the woman's gun was found.
Another policeman pulled out a shotgun quick as ever. Then another cop hit the woman's gun with his hand, just to brush it aside,
and the gun went off in the air. So the woman's gun getting fired
during the arrest complicated everything with the case. The court
appointed a lawyer for Richard, but I could see it was all gonna be
uphill. In the end they gave him a "ten, split three" sentence, meaning he was gonna be locked up for three years mandatory and it
could stretch to ten years depending on his behavior. Richard was
set to do some time.

They put him in Draper, a class C prison. I followed his case in bits and pieces from then on because the chaplain would phone me up from time to time and we talked. Within two weeks of landing in Draper, Richard got himself into a drug class. That musta been an act of mercy because Richard needed it for sure, and I heard it usually takes eighteen months before someone can get into those. Two months after that Richard passed the drug class and was sent to Elmore, a minimum-security prison downstate. He got on maintenance crew there. His time was mostly spent outside working around the grounds, which I guess ain't too bad for prison life, but I knowed that prison was still prison, and that he was still locked on the inside. One day while in Elmore, Richard called me and asked if I could come down and see him. I hesitated. Wasn't nothing left to say to him, I figured.

"So what you want to talk to me about, anyway?" I asked. I had decided to go down there and we was sitting together in the prison visiting area.

Richard swallowed a few times. His hands were shaking. "They offered me a work-release program, ma'am. That's some good news for me, but there's a problem."

"What's that?"

"Well." I could tell he was searching for the right words. "Before they release me, I need to have a job."

Was he serious? I knew what he was asking, and it was gonna take some wrestling in my mind to sort through what I needed to say next. He was a captive and was calling on me to proclaim liberty. Those old familiar words from Isaiah 61 started pressing on my mind. Those were the terms I had founded my restaurant on, the terms Sophia had pressed me to keep. That's why I had chosen to run my restaurant my way in the first place, so it could become a place of second chances. Yet I didn't feel like moving. This situation with Richard was different.

This one was his third chance. And it was real probable that there'd be more trouble after this. This one also felt different because it was personal. Richard had robbed me, robbed my restaurant, taken my car, and lied about most things, I was pretty sure. He still needed some time inside to think things over. He deserved to be where he was. He did. That was the voice of law talking.

Sitting in the jail I started getting this image in my head. It was real faint, but I could just make it out. The vision was of a wealthy father. His son had wished him dead. The boy had run off and squandered his inheritance. Everything valuable was soon lost or destroyed. Now the boy was broke and eating slop with pigs; he knew even his father's hired helpers ate better than that. That's when the boy wanted to come home, while he was still a long way off.

"Richard, how long you been in jail now, anyway?" I asked. I spoke slowly, still not sure of what I was needing to do.

"Nine months."

"So you got most of your years left to go, is that right?

He nodded.

The father was running, running. The father was running straight toward the boy. On that long road of third and fourth and seventh and twentieth chances, that father ran toward the prodigal son with his arms wide open. That was the same scandalous love that had been extended to me to cover all the mistakes I had ever made. Those were the same scandalous terms I was invited to extend to others.

"Richard, I want to say something to you, and I never want you to forget it."

"Yes, ma'am."

My voice was low. "Welcome home, son. Welcome home."

17

Martha's Place

THE YEARS PASSED BY, LIKE they're so bound to do and keep doing.

In fact, it's been more than twenty years since I first opened my restaurant doors. Oooh, the heaps of good food we done served up in this place. Baked chicken and grilled steak and sizzled catfish and seafood gumbo and buttered lima beans and collard greens and so much more. And the quality of folks who came through those doors and keep coming today—all folks. Folks needing help. Folks just looking to eat. Rich folks. Poor folks. Regular folks. Famous folks.

Here's how things have wrapped up in these past years of success.

My daddy came to work with me pretty early on. He came to the restaurant with his strong factory hands, and side by side we worked together in that place of dreams. He was so proud of what we were doing. The work was more like play with him around. He was laughing most days toward the end, not in a crazy way, although he developed Alzheimer's in his last days. It was more just a constant gentle laughing, like he was savoring his last moments of being close to the folks he loved most. Daddy loved to tell jokes, and he loved to play checkers, so he combined the two often. He'd do something to distract you and then fix the check-erboard and jump two or three while you weren't looking. Daddy went on to glory in 1998 at age eighty-nine, and before that, even on his most forgetful days with Alzheimer's, whenever they brought him by the restaurant he always recognized it and knew where he was. All the family was surrounding him when he passed, hold-ing his hands as he crossed the Jordan through that shoulder-deep water. He was stooped in body but full of love and joy and years of spirit, that was Daddy.

My mama came to help in the restaurant, too. A lot of my reci-pes began with her in those early years. Sallie Bell Hawkins had a way of setting things straight and helping folks get set right and she talked many times about the great sense of pride she had in watching her daughter open up a restaurant of her own. My mama loved everybody she met, and though she loved everybody, she never made a person feel lumped in together with others—we was all individuals to her. When she passed at age ninety-two we held a graveside service over at Eastwood Cemetery so all who knew her well could come. Cars were parked all over the lawn and all the way up and down Wares Ferry Road. Folks said they had never seen such a large graveside service before. My mother passed into yonder with a prayer on her lips and a smile for the Lord. She also left a legacy of raising right 12 children, 67 grandchildren, 160 great-grand-children, and 33 great-great-grandchildren. That's a total of 272 folks living on to carry her influence.

My sister Willela went into the hospital at age forty-five for something or other and the doctor looked things over and said she could go home. Willela was up right away, talking and laughing, but in an hour she was gone. It was a stroke, real unexpected, and we miss her much.

My brother Edward never did go into the military like he talked about that day back in Trenholm Court. He went into food sales and did well at it, working in that occupation for years. Then he came to work for me and managed the restaurant for a spell. After he retired he became an ordained minister and is still working in that vocation today, helping folks out wherever he's able—prison ministry mostly. Edward's as quick with the kindness today as he ever was, and sometimes I wished we could still go out and play stickball on the front road like we used to, but we're both getting on in years and stickball is mostly behind us now.

My brother Henry worked for the school system in Montgomery and later in Madison. He had been drawing and painting since he was a little boy and later he got his master's degree in art. Some of his paintings hang in the restaurant today, and you'll see them there if y'all ever come and dine. We have a real good relationship and always have.

My sister Rosa came to work for me in the restaurant about seventeen years ago and she's still working there today. When she first came she said, "Just show me what to do," so I showed her how to make cakes and pies and she's been making them ever since. She takes extra pride in her work and you can't mess with her pies and cakes, no sir. If you try to take them out of the oven for her she'll shout, "Don't touch!" and won't let you near. It's really been a blessing to have her so close. I love Rosa dearly like I love all my brothers and sisters. A lot of them have helped out at the restaurant from time to time throughout the different seasons. It's been good to work alongside family because you learn each other and have a closer relationship that way. It's been a lot of fun and I'm blessed to have my family be a part of what I'm doing. My sister Georgia works regularly with me in the restaurant today also, and it's real fun to have her there, and my sister Alberta and I are what you'd call prayer partners today—we get together quite often and lift up whatever needs lifting to our Lord.

Most of my brothers and sisters live in Montgomery today and we get together whenever we can. There ain't no formal invitations that go out or nothing. We just call everybody up and say, Hey we're all meeting at so-and-so's house. Then we all get together and eat. Someone's always bound to get forgotten in the calling up. Come midsupper someone will say, Hey, where's so-and-so? I thought you called him. Well, I thought *you* called him. And it's funny after all these years because we don't ever aim to leave nobody out. But true as true when that person finds out that everybody got together without him then he's steaming mad at the rest of us for a while. But that's the way it is when you're part of a large family. That's just the way it is.

Just the other day we all gathered over at Reginald's house for supper, and I don't think anyone was missing the fun that night. My son's doing real well for himself today, working as a loan officer and married to a beautiful woman named Krista. They have a fine daughter, Brianna, who just got accepted to Vanderbilt University. That's what we were celebrating that night. Reginald's got a spread that's big enough to handle everybody, and he barbecued us up some ribs and made baked beans and tossed up a delicious green salad and for dessert there was red velvet cake all around. Halfway through supper, Reginald raised his glass and made a toast. "You know, we always had love," he said. "At times we had nothing, but we always had love. That got us to the point we are now."

We all clinked our glasses to that.

Quintin and his pretty wife, Natalyn, were there. They've got two little ones, a boy Christian and a girl Carsyn, who scampered in and out and was still talking about all the fine things they got for Christmas this year. After college, Quint came and worked in my restaurant and became the manager there for a spell although he was destined to keep going other places in his career. He looks back on those days now with fondness, saying how he really learned diplomacy in a restaurant—to listen to what people are like and respect their differences, to wait on them, to pay attention to their mannerisms, to flex to their differing moods and attitudes. Today, all that diplomacy training has paid off and Quint works as a lobbyist. He's a managing partner in his firm, the McWhorter Group, and stays real busy in that challenging role of helping people and companies work things out. Quint's real smart and he's living in a fine house up on the hill as well. I'm real proud of how he's doing. Real proud.

My youngest, Nyrone, drove down from Memphis to the supper with his lovely wife, Yolanda. That's where they stay and it ain't too far away from us. They've been married six years now and have got a sweet young daughter, Nyia. Back in college days, Nyrone was heavily recruited for football and played for Memphis State, but he broke his ankle his junior year and wasn't able to play again. The voice of love had other plans for him. For some time he wandered in his journey, unsure of where to land. Out of college he worked for the airlines and was in my restaurant one day when he met one of my most faithful customers who had brought along her grown-up daughter. Well, the sparks started flying, for that grown-up daughter was soon to become Nyrone's wife, and that's how they met, right there in my restaurant. That good woman musta been exactly who Nyrone needed to help find his way because today he's an ordained minister and just started up a group home for boys where he's the director. The children who come to him are said to be severely emotionally disturbed, and his presence provides a strong male role model to replace the fathers they often never knew.

My oldest son Shawn was really happy because he grew six inches after graduating from college, which is a running joke in our house 'cause he was always complaining he was too short. He joined the Birmingham police department his senior year of college and finished his degree while working a full-time job. Then in 1991 he was recruited by the FBI. That's when he got his picture taken shaking hands with the president, the day he became sworn in as a federal agent. Today he's a supervisor at the bureau and is in charge of a task force. They work gangs and violent crime, and are doing real good work making this country a safer place for all. Seventeen years ago Shawn married a beautiful woman named Sharon and today they have two dazzling daughters, Martina and Gabrielle, who simply mean the world to me.

The restaurant's done well for itself and I've made some money over the years, though it seems to come and go and be gone more than it stays. For a while I lived in a big fancy house but it was just me rambling all alone there and I didn't need all that space, so now I'm back living in an apartment. It's in a new section of town and it's just the amount of room I need.

I haven't kept much in contact with Sylvester or James, two of the daddies of my boys. There's no animosity there. It's just something that happened, you know. None of that was nobody's fault. I think that's how everybody feels with the passing of time.

My ex-husband Reuben and I are still good friends. We always were. His mama and daddy were always like another set of folks to me. After getting out of the military, Reuben worked the pipelines up in Alaska for years, where he still owns a house. He spends summers up there these days but stays in Mississippi during the rest of the year. We talk on the phone about once a month.

Folks sometimes ask me if I'll ever get involved romantically again. Well, I'm open to that direction but it hasn't happened because I've been so busy working and enjoying what I'm doing. After all that drama I went through in my younger years, I determined to be the best mom I could be and devoted myself to my sons and later to my grandkids. It don't bother me that I'm not in a relationship. I'm okay. I'm not desperate, and I'm not seeking. I know exactly what kind of man I'd like and he hasn't come along yet. I believe that when he does, then boom—it'll happen. The lightbulb will come on and shine bright all around.

Here's what's been happening to the other folks mentioned in this book.

When Richard was set free from jail back in 1994, he came back to Martha's Place on a work-release program and has been doing real well ever since. Richard has been clean and sober and hasn't had so much as a brush with the law or drugs in all the years that've passed. Richard worked with me in the restaurant for two years after getting released, then he trained to be a machinist, which is what he's doing today. He still stops in at the restaurant and helps out with catering from time to time. We always have a good talk when he does.

Sophia Bracy Harris is still executive director of FOCAL and continues with her serving ways, helping folks out wherever she is able to make a difference. I never did mention about her that she knew the facts of getting kicked down firsthand, which makes her story even better because of all the good she went on to make with her life. Back in the 1960s, her parents' home got firebombed because Sophia was one of the first blacks to attend her neighborhood high school. We've all come a long way since then.

Speaking of that, I won't tell you who I voted for in the last presidential election, because either way there's bound to be folks who disagree and I aim to be friends with everybody. But I will say this. I was mighty proud of the journey President Obama has been on to get where he is today. Born in 1961, he's about the same age and stage as my sons, and you have to think that by the time the young Barack Obama started elementary school in Hawaii, if he had been living in Alabama then he wouldn't have been able to attend school alongside of white children. *Brown v. Board of Education* passed in 1954 and it legally ended segregation, but it wasn't fully implemented in Alabama schools until the end of the 1960s. That's part of the good change that has happened in our generation—this generation—so much powerful change has come through at last.

By law I ain't allowed to give any specifics regarding the folks I knowed at Greil because everything's anonymous over there, and that's fine. For some time I stayed in contact with the folks I had knowed when I was there, but folks drift to other things and I'm not keeping up with any of them no more except one. Maybe you can guess who it is. This one young lady calls me quite a bit and stops by the restaurant whenever she's able. She's in and out of depression but she's got spirit and she's strong, and I ain't stopped praying for the Lord's plans for her life.

The good administrators at Greil have had me come back there several times to speak to the patients more formal-like. They had an annual meeting up at Shocco Springs and got me to speak at it. For a while I was on the board of the Montgomery Mental Health Association and was also sitting on the Montgomery Mental Health Authority, the governing body that makes most of the decisions for mental health care in this area. It takes an appointment by the county commissioner to sit on the authority, and I got that and felt good about that. A couple of years back I was also a United Way ambassador and went around and represented the mental health side of things for them.

I closed the second restaurant location at Hull Hope when the hotel got sold over there and became something else. Never did open up another location, but we've branched out in other ways. We've got a government contract to cater food for the work-release program at the county jail, feeding the bodies of the souls in captivity there. Then lately we've been working on a frozen foods line that should be carried in grocery stores real soon. Mostly I've been putting my energy into developing a program called Martha Hawkins Ministries. We work with low-income kids and single parents mostly and aim to let folks know what they're capable of doing. I think a lot of folks feel trapped by their life circumstances; they feel like they can't go no farther or do nothing else. So I get groups of moms and kids coming in, and we serve them and feed them and talk. It's all about loving folks. That's why the Lord allowed me to go through a lot of those hard things and then be successful—it wasn't just for me, but to help others, to let them know that if God can do it for me, then he can do it for them.

Along those lines, my public speaking has taken off real fine. Today, I do a lot of speaking for the Gideons International. What with me finding that Gideon Bible in the drawer back at Greil and it having such a powerful hand in changing my life for the better, I figured I could give much back to the organization that had done me and so many others so much good.

Word tends to get around when you're speaking, and altogether I've spoken in thirty-six different states now, at colleges, clubs, women's groups, sororities, churches, business organizations, and more. I'm doing quite a bit of corporate speaking these days, too. Recently I was the keynote speaker for a get-together at the Eli Lilly pharmaceutical company, and doing corporate speaking is really how this book came to be. I had spoken up at Sam's Club, part of the Wal-Mart Corporation, and I guess the CEO there really liked what I had to say. Each time he came to the area he would make a point to bring his team to the restaurant for lunch. He is a truly good-hearted man who cares about the folks who work for the company, and it's clear they care a lot about him too. He said, "Martha, if there's ever anything I can do to help you, please let me know." I thanked him and knew in my spirit he meant what he said. Anyway, he encouraged me to put my stories down on paper, and that's how this book project first got rolling.

I don't take credit for any of that goodness—books and speaking and traveling and whatnot. I must be clear here. All this success doesn't flow from my power. It's the voice of love moving in my life. All I know to do today is to keep stepping into his promises for me. He's good and he's got good places for me to go. That's the real story of my life. Heaven is waiting for me like it's waiting for you, and you're invited to this party because of the scandalous terms of grace.

You know, I don't ever take notes up with me when I speak. God trained me to depend on him for my words. I've tried to write things down beforehand but I'm never able to look at my notes. I just go where I'm supposed to go and start speaking from the heart. The words that flow from me must be okay words because folks keep asking me back to speak. I never take credit for how those words being spoken might affect a person's life. All my messages usually start the same. All odds were stacked against me but God had a different plan, and all things are possible for those who believe. I go from there.

So that's about all I want to say now. I've got some cooking to do and I need to be wrapping this up. Let me be praying for you. Right now, in fact—God ain't bound by time or distance or the pages of a book. *O Gracious God, may you bless anybody who's reading this book. May your face shine upon this person whoever they may be. May you give them peace and bless their family and bring glory and goodness and hope and promise into their life. Amen, and for all times, amen.* Will you shout that with me like you're in a gospel choir? *Amen!*

By the way, the food is always available, always piping hot, always comforting, always tasting good all the time. Martha's Place is still open for business, so y'all come on down to 458 Sayre Street if you're ever in Montgomery. Let Martha fix you up some real good soul food. It's mighty tasty, so y'all come now and eat up, y'hear?

Recipes for Tasting and Seeing from

Martha's Place Restaurant

SALLIE HAWKINS'S CORN BREAD

1½ cups self-rising cornmeal
½ cup self-rising flour
¼ cup sugar
2 eggs
2 tablespoons mayonnaise
1 cup buttermilk
4 tablespoons shortening, melted
½ cup water

1. Preheat the oven to 425 degrees.
2. Combine all the ingredients in a medium mixing bowl. Stir with a wooden spoon until thoroughly blended.
3. Pour the mixture into a well-greased skillet and bake 35 minutes, until golden brown.

Serves 12

PORK CHOP CASSEROLE

6 pork chops
1 tablespoon cooking oil
3 large potatoes, peeled and sliced
½ pound carrots, sliced in disks
1 large onion, sliced
one 10½-ounce can condensed mushroom soup

1. Preheat the oven to 350 degrees.
2. Heat the oil in a skillet and brown the pork chops on both sides.
3. Place the pork chops in a 2-quart casserole dish. Add the potatoes, carrots, onions, and mushroom soup. Cover with lid or foil.
4. Bake 45 minutes.

Serves 6

SOUTHERN BAKED CATFISH

6 fillet catfish fillets
2 tablespoons melted butter
½ teaspoon garlic powder
½ teaspoon dried basil (or 1 teaspoon fresh)
½ teaspoon dried oregano
½ teaspoon black pepper
½ teaspoon salt
½ teaspoon dry thyme
1½ cups crushed dry cornflakes

1. Preheat the oven to 350 degrees.
2. In a medium bowl, mix together the herbs and cornflakes.
3. Place the catfish in a 2-quart casserole dish. Brush with the melted butter. Cover with the cornflake mixture.
4. Bake 15–20 minutes.

Serves 6

MARTHA'S MAC & CHEESE

2 pounds elbow macaroni
1 stick (½ cup) margarine
2½ cups milk
1 pound sharp cheddar cheese, shredded
½ pound mild cheddar cheese, shredded
one 10½-ounce can condensed cheddar cheese soup
salt and pepper, to taste
4 eggs, beaten

1. Preheat the oven to 350 degrees.
2. Cook the macaroni according to package directions. Drain.
3. In a large bowl, combine the macaroni, margarine, milk, cheeses, soup, and salt and pepper. Stir in the beaten eggs.
4. Pour the mixture in a greased casserole dish.
5. Bake 35 minutes.

Serves 8

BRIANNA'S UNFORGETABLE RICE

1 cup diced celery

1 cup green onion (scallions), sliced

1 cup chopped green pepper

1 teaspoon poultry seasoning

1 teaspoon salt

½ teaspoon pepper

3 cups chicken broth

2 cups long-grain rice (white or brown)

1 tablespoon pimientos

1. Preheat the oven to 350 degrees.
2. In a large nonstick skillet, over medium-high heat, sauté the celery, green onions, and green pepper until tender.
3. Add the pimientos, poultry seasoning, salt and pepper, and broth.
4. Put the rice in shallow 2-quart baking dish: Add the hot broth mixture. Cover.
5. Bake 30 minutes, or until the rice is tender and all the liquid is absorbed.

Serves 8

CHEESY SCALLOPED POTATOES

4 large white potatoes, peeled and sliced
1 large onion, chopped
1 cup milk
1¼ cups shredded cheddar cheese
½ teaspoon salt
½ teaspoon pepper

1. Preheat the oven to 350 degrees.
2. Place the potatoes and onions in a saucepan. Cover with water. Boil for 20 minutes, or until tender. Drain.
3. In a greased casserole dish, combine the potatoes and the remaining ingredients.
4. Bake 30 minutes.

Serves 8

FRIED GREEN TOMATOES

4 large green tomatoes
1 cup yellow cornmeal
½ cup flour
salt and pepper, to taste
1 cup cooking oil

1. Cut the tomatoes into ½-inch slices.
2. Combine the cornmeal, flour, salt, and pepper in a bowl. Coat both sides of the tomato slices with the mixture.
3. Heat half the oil in a large skillet. Over medium heat, brown the tomato slices on both sides. You'll need to do this in two batches; the tomatoes should not overlap.
4. Drain on paper towels.

Serves 6

MARTINA'S DELIGHT

20-ounce loaf white bread
1 can condensed milk
16-ounce bag shredded coconut

1. Preheat the oven to 350 degrees.
2. Cut the crusts off the bread. Cut each slice into three strips.
3. Dip the bread into the milk and then roll in the coconut.
4. Place on a greased cookie sheet and bake 15 minutes.

Serves about 12

PERFECT PECAN PIE

3 eggs
¾ cup *Karo Syrup*
¾ cup sugar
1 teaspoon vanilla extract
2 tablespoons melted butter
1 cup pecan halves
1 prepared pie shell

1. Preheat the oven to 350 degrees.
2. In a mixing bowl, beat the eggs and syrup. Add the sugar, vanilla, and butter. Mix well. Stir in the pecans.
3. Bake the pie shell 10 minutes.
4. Pour the filling into the shell.
5. Lower the oven to 325 degrees. Bake 1 hour.

Serves 8

A note from Martha: You can of course make your own piecrust, but a prepared shell is just as good, and it saves time.

CALVIN PRYOR'S WHIPPED CREAM POUND CAKE

3 cups all-purpose flour or cake flour
1 teaspoon baking powder
1 cup butter, softened
3 cups sugar
1 teaspoon vanilla extract
6 eggs, room temperature
1 cup (8 ounces) whipping (heavy) cream (not ultra-pasturized)

1. Preheat the oven to 350 degrees.
2. Sift together the flour and baking powder. Set aside.
3. Beat the butter in a large bowl with an electric mixer (on medium to high speed) until soft. Gradually add the sugar and beat for about 6 minutes, or until very light and fluffy.
4. Add the vanilla extract, then one egg at a time, beating on low to medium speed for 1 minute after each addition. Scrape the side of bowl often.

5. Gradually add the flour mixture and beat until well mixed.
6. Whip the cream until almost stiff. Stir gently into the batter and mix well.
7. Grease and lightly flour a loaf pan. Add the butter.
8. Bake 55 to 65 minutes, or until a cake tester comes out clean.
9. Cool the cake in the pan on a rack for 10 minutes. Remove the cake from pan and cool completely on the rack.

About 24 slices

Acknowledgments

I THANK GOD FOR SHAWN, Quint, Reginald, and Nyrone for being the motivating force to help me want to keep on fighting to live. You have made me one proud mom. You are the wind beneath my wings.

To Sharon, Krista, Natalyn, and Yolanda, I couldn't have been more blessed with four great daughters than I've been with all of you. I love you deeply. Thanks for six wonderful grandchildren—Briana, Martina, Gabrielle, Christian, Carsyn, and Nyia. God has truly blessed me by having each of you be part of my life.

Rosalee, I never could have made it if you weren't there with me. You have been my support and my prayer partner. You are the glue that holds everything together.

Much thanks goes out to my wonderful brothers and sisters: Georgia, Alice, Alberta, Henry, Willie Jr., Tommy, Edward, Howard, Wylie, and to the memory of Willela. I love you all. Let's get together real soon for dinner.

Thanks to all of the I Love You Martha committee for your support, help, and love.

Mike Jenkins, thanks for being a friend and always believing in me. Marty Ramsey, I think you were my first customer ever. Thanks for your unswerving support throughout the years.

My unending gratitude extends to Doug McMillon—this wouldn't have happened without you.

Thank you to the Gideons International for placing the word of God in hospitals, hotels, and all over. Your work revolutionized my whole life.

Thanks to Dr. John Zeigler and Allen Steward for the great job you're doing with mental health.

Thanks to Dr. Steven Paul and the Eli Lilly Pharmaceutical company for your support.

A special thanks to the Federation of Child Care Centers of Alabama (FOCAL) and the women of the Southern Rural Black Women's Initiative (SRBWI).

To my agent Terry Davis from Davis & Hatcher, LLC, to Greg Johnson from the WordServe Literary Group, to Marcus Brotherton, I had a wonderful time collaborating with you. And to editor Sulay Hernandez, Shawna Lietzke, and all the team at Simon & Schuster, thanks for believing in this project from moment one. It truly has been fun.

Thank you, Montgomery, for giving me an opportunity to live out my dreams.

There are so many other folks I need to thank. I know I'm leaving out lots of names, but you know who you are, and you know what you mean to me: I love you all. If y'all feel left out, just come on by for a free scoop of bread pudding. I'll fix you up.

About
Martha Hawkins
Ministries

Martha Hawkins Ministries exists
to share hope with the hopeless
and give advantage to the disadvantaged
through the love of Jesus Christ.

We do this by
encouraging,
motivating,
teaching,
training, and
empowering
people to bring about change
from the inside out.

Contact us at

Martha Hawkins Ministries
488 Sayre Street
Montgomery, AL 36104
334-263-9135 (restaurant)
www.marthahawkinsministries.org

About the Authors

MARTHA HAWKINS'S life is a testament to faith and dreams, love and hope, and hard work. Born the tenth of twelve children in Montgomery at the height of the civil rights movement, Martha overcame poverty and episodes of deep depression to become a successful restaurateur and inspirational speaker. Today, her restaurant Martha's Place is a nationally known stop for anyone who visits the Deep South and is a culinary fixture of life for Montgomery residents. Her cooking, restaurant, life story, and inspirational words have been featured in many national publications including *The New York Times, O, The Oprah Magazine, Southern Living, Essence,* and *Guideposts.*

MARCUS BROTHERTON is the author or coauthor of nineteen books. He has collaborated with Dr. Nancy Heche (mother of Anne Heche), international humanitarian Susan Scott Krabacher, and most recently on *We Who Are Alive and Remain,* a compilation memoir with twenty of the original Band of Brothers.

Printed in the USA
CPSIA information can be obtained
at www.ICGtesting.com
BVHW071136300723
667922BV00005B/8